Cowdray
and
Easebourne

Andrew Guyatt and Vic Mitchell

MP Middleton Press

Foreword

As a child Easebourne for me was one of those villages you passed through as you headed for the coast; yellow doors and window frames, cottages nestled in between more recent dwellings and the overriding sense of community and busy life. Being Vicar here now for a few years has given me the chance to **be** in this place rather than pass through. I have discovered that this is a very important place, not only because of its history and beautiful surroundings, but because of the people who live and work here.

This book gathers together in a very thorough and engaging style the different elements of Easebourne that make it so special; from the historic Priory Church to the warm and friendly village store, from the polo fields to the three schools that have taught generations of villagers. There is much to celebrate and much to read about this important place, holding such diverse subjects as a communication mast and a workhouse in one publication; who wouldn't be intrigued?

Derek Welsman
(Vicar 2002 -   )
St.Mary's Church Easebourne

Published February 2007

ISBN   *1 904474 96 9*
             978 1 904474 96 8

© *Middleton Press, 2007*

Design Deborah Esher

Published by
        Middleton Press
        Easebourne Lane
        Midhurst
        West Sussex
        GU29 9AZ
Tel: 01730 813169
Fax: 01730 812601
Email: info@middletonpress.co.uk
www.middletonpress.co.uk

Printed & bound by Biddles Ltd, Kings Lynn

Contents

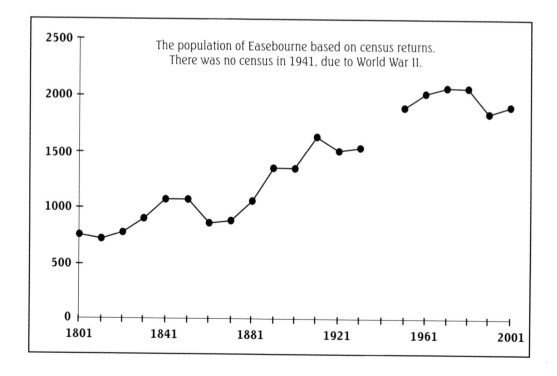

The population of Easebourne based on census returns.
There was no census in 1941, due to World War II.

Pronunciations

Judiths Glover's 1975 book, *The Place Names of Sussex* quotes "Ezbourne". We decided that a survey would best indicate present usage. The use of "bun" or "burn" has not been found elsewhere in England, although is common in Scotland. It is thought to have originated in the days of the illiterate and has been perpetuated by a few.

	Es-bun	Es-born	Ease-born
Primary School	0	159	0
Intermediate School	3	276	1
Conifers School	0	80	0
Easebourne Parish Council	12	0	0
Parochial Church Council	4	10	0
Midhurst Society	14	30	1
Easebourne Lunch Club	14	27	0
Totals	47	582	2
Percentage	7.5%	92.2%	0.3%

Acknowledgements and Introduction

We are very grateful for the assistance received from those recorded here and in the sources. Others have helped in varying ways but it is impossible to record everyone's name here and we apologise to any who feel they have been overlooked. Our appreciation is sincere. Lord Egremont of Petworth must be acknowledged in conjunction with the West Sussex County Council Records Office for access to archives. We also thank S.S.Davies (Midhurst Intermediate School information), C. Dudeney (Postal data), Emma Esher (recent photographs), M.J.Freeman (sourcing), Christine Maynard (Fernhurst Archive), D. Rudwick (historic photographs), J. Stringer (local records), R.Taylor (leisure subjects), W.Lewis née Pearce (local information), J.Magilton (early history), J.Wildman (Cowdray Estate archaeology) and I.Brown (Henley illustrations). Other helpers are noted at the end of the relevant chapters.

Local historians are undertaking further research, notably in the medieval period, and thus comments herein draw upon published information, which may be subject to amendment in the future.

We apologise to those in organisations, trades or industries who feel under-represented in this volume. We have endeavoured to concentrate on those areas of life that have been particularly notable in, or exclusive to, the parish. Our gratitude to the many folk, too numerous to mention, who have added details or provided notes to add to our initial draft, is very sincere.

About the Authors

Dr Andrew Guyatt moved to the parish in 1975 to carry out research at the Midhurst Medical Institute in respiratory physiology, publishing a number of scientific papers.

Dr Vic Mitchell came to Easebourne in 1962 to practise dentistry and also produced some biochemistry papers. He co-authored **Branch Lines to Midhurst** in 1981, establishing Middleton Press to publish it.

Both authors soon realised that their home village had a unique and fascinating history, only ever fragmentally recorded. A close friendship developed, largely due to their shared joy in the Christian faith.

While involved in the Bible College, Andrew Guyatt began to unravel the complex story of the former workhouse in which it was located and his publication on this topic prompted Vic Mitchell to realise that his oft repeated dream of a history of their village could be created around this. Andrew Guyatt responded by writing chapters 2 to 9 plus parts of 11, 13 and 14 of this volume, while Vic Mitchell has compiled much of the others, along with the captions to the maps and photographs. His family business has published this book.

❧ Maps ❧

✒ 1. The Beginnings ✒

The sand and sandstone on which the parish stands is sedimentary, this meaning that it was formed as a sediment at the bottom of the sea. This layer was subsequently overlaid by Chalk and other deposits. However, these were eventually eroded and cut back southwards, the Chalk's northern limit being at Cocking.

All the layers were subjected to pressure from the south, which resulted in the formation of a slight dome of which the North and South Downs form the remains of its outer edges. This pressure was due to tectonic plate movement when Africa collided with Europe, forced up the Alps and also generated the incline we encounter travelling north in the parish, over the Lower Greensand.

This deposit contains thin layers of ironstones, seen as rusty stripes in the cuttings for roads. This is impermeable to water and its configuration in the northern part of the parish has given rise to a perpetual spring of fresh water. This forms the Es Bourne (stream) and it is this which attracted habitation. It still flows close to Easebourne Street. These highways, along with the Dodsley Lane length of the A286, are typical water cut sunken roads of the sedimentary deposits. They often return to being rivers after periods of heavy rain.

Farming seems to have been practised in the area since about 4000BC. Polished axe heads were found near King Edward VII Hospital and were dated as Neolithic. The Bronze Age (1500 to 750BC) may be represented by a burial mound (barrow) near Little Common Reservoir, but no sites of occupation seem to have been reported.

This location is known as Wheelbarrow Castle, but no trace of a burial barrow or a castle remain. However, both are usually built on elevated ground with good visibility, such as this. It is possible that a wooden castle was built on the site of a wheel-shaped barrow and that any reusable material was used to develop the village. A local postman remembers that in the 1920s there was a mound "about 3 yards high and a dip of around 1 yard, nearby". There is another Wheelbarrow Castle, two miles southeast of Leominster.

It is interesting to note that a straight path still exists almost all the way from the village centre to the site of Verdley Castle, just in the parish of Fernhurst, Its remains are shown on early OS maps and the path aligns with North Mill bridge.

Applying a rule to the map of the parish will reveal other alignments, which may have historic significance. A **parallel** route can be found running north from the Ruins along The Chase to the two hunting parks, North Park and West Heath. Parallel lines are often deemed significant in the early history of other parts of the country.

Evidence of Roman occupation is unsubstantiated and claims of a Roman pavement in Henley seem to have no basis. The straight section of the A286 appears to be Roman, but it is from the turnpike era, the earlier curving alignments being evident where coppicing has taken place east of the road. (The main Roman road north of Chichester ran via Milland).

Aspects of the survey of England by King William I are constantly disputed, even its title: Doomsday or Doomesday. Neither Midhurst or Easebourne are listed as communities; some think deliberately while others consider they have been lost. There is no doubt that the latter is mentioned as a Hundred, a sub-division of a shire. A population of a little over 1000 is estimated, this excluding slaves, the number of villages being 12. The book was published in 1086.

It is thought that Easebourne had been an important place in Anglo-Saxon times and that a minster existed here to serve the district.

Sources
Lawrence, B. "The Missing People of Doomsday". (Midhurst Heritage Issue No. 2.)
Magilton, J. and Thomas, S. "Midhurst" 2001
Murrant, EG. (Interviewed - aged 96 years)

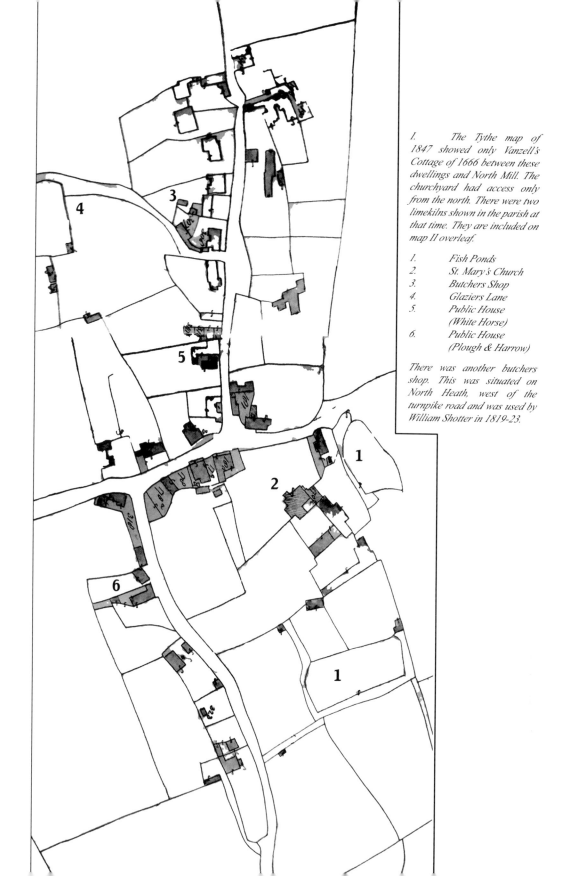

1.   *The Tythe map of 1847 showed only Vanzell's Cottage of 1666 between these dwellings and North Mill. The churchyard had access only from the north. There were two limekilns shown in the parish at that time. They are included on map II overleaf.*

1.   *Fish Ponds*
2.   *St. Mary's Church*
3.   *Butchers Shop*
4.   *Glaziers Lane*
5.   *Public House*
    (White Horse)
6.   *Public House*
    (Plough & Harrow)

There was another butchers shop. This was situated on North Heath, west of the turnpike road and was used by William Shotter in 1819-23.

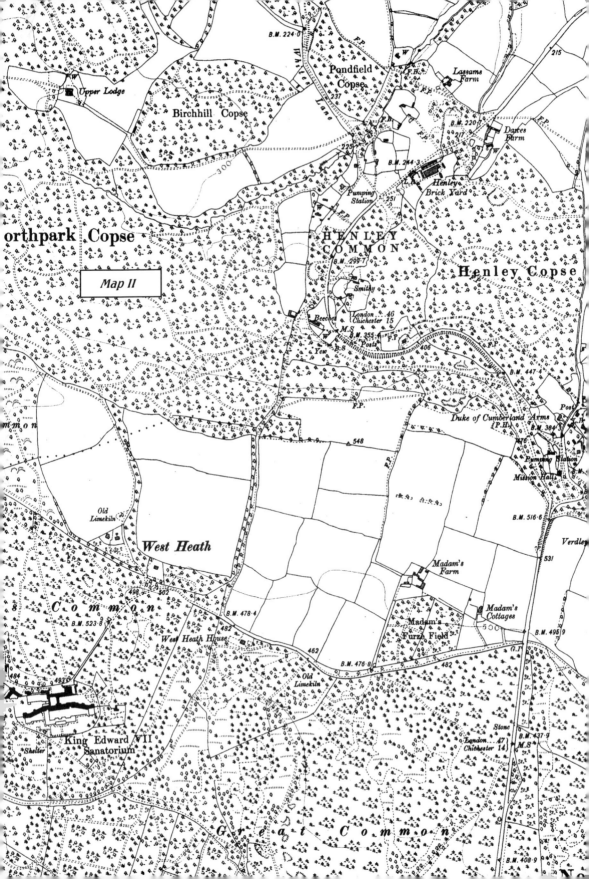

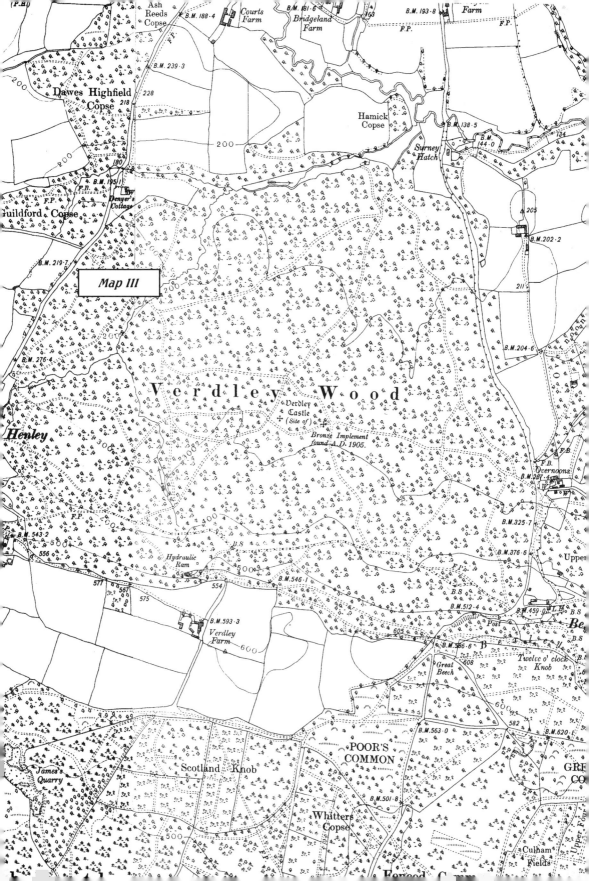

Map IV

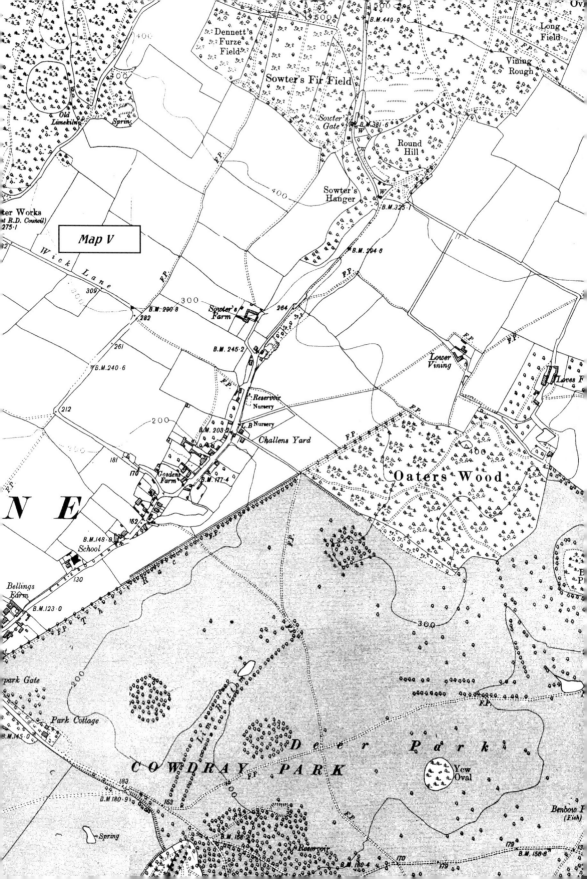

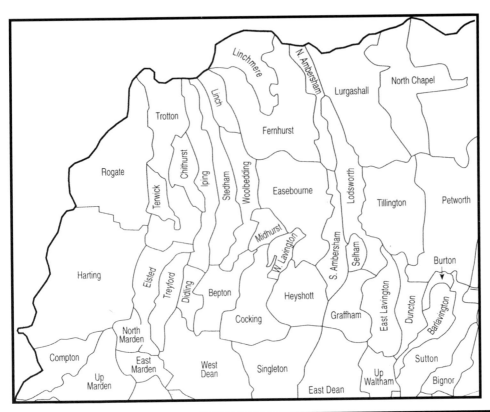

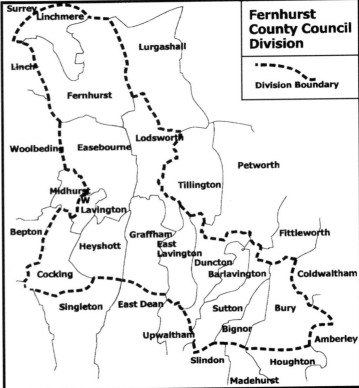

VI. Easebourne and its adjacent parishes in 1890. North and South Ambersham were outliers of Sheet and were thus part of Hampshire. They were later incorporated into parishes to the east, not Easebourne.

VII. From May 2005, Easebourne came into the Fernhurst Division of the county, which excluded Midhurst. The thin lines are parish boundaries.

Fernhurst County Council Division

Division Boundary

◈ 2. Cowdray ◈

St Ann's Hill

The story of Cowdray House began across the river Rother on St Ann's Hill. This vantage point appears to have been named after St. Denis, a third century Bishop of Paris, but according to Magilton the name was corrupted to Tan's Hill and later to St. Ann's.

The first building may have been a timber structure on an earth mound, constructed by Roger de Montgomery. He was a close friend of William the Conqueror who granted him extensive lands in the west of Sussex, known as the Rape of Arundel, from which the Rape of Chichester was later divided.

When Henry I became king in 1100, Roger's eldest son Robert, rebelled and his lands were confiscated. Midhurst was given to Savaric Fitz Cana who married Muriel, granddaughter of Humphrey de Bohun, and the family adopted this surname.

The de Bohuns prospered and the castle was rebuilt in stone as a fortified manor house, although the main family residence was at Ford. A descendant, John, served Edward I in Wales and Ireland and around 1270 gave the king a loan. But he then had financial problems, and by 1284 had entered into an arrangement with Anthony Bek, Bishop of Durham, to act as his administrator.

Most of John's male descendants died young, so Bishop Bek continued to act until his death in 1311. Some of his servants may have demolished the manor house since in 1316 the de Bohuns brought an action claiming his agents had pulled down a hall worth £50, a chamber worth £62, two chapels worth £5 each, a kitchen worth £6/13/4 and a granary worth £3/6/8! But some buildings still remained 40 years later.

La Coudreye

By the 13th century the de Bohuns had two parks in Easebourne. One known as La Sengle or Cengle (probably meaning thicket) was north of the Petworth road and 87 trees were cut down here while Bishop Bek was in charge. The other park, La Codray, (French for hazel), lay to the south.

Sometime before 1317, the family decided to move across the river and erect a house on the flood plain. However the new site lacked the security of a castle, as John's widow Joanna was to find out.

In that year, she complained that Edward St.John and William Avenal with other evildoers had broken down the gates and the drawbridge of her mansion at Easebourne, entering her house, leading away a horse and removing other goods and chattels to the value of £100. Three years later she complained of a similar attack on her house, which was now named as La Coudreye. However it is possible that this action was taken by her late husband's creditors to reclaim some of what was owed them.

From the reference to a drawbridge, it seems the building had a moat, but despite four archaeological surveys, the site has not been identified. It probably lies beneath the present ruins; during excavations in 1913, a pillar was discovered which was typical of 13th century work.

Sir David Owen

The last male de Bohun, John, died about 1494. Six years earlier, his daughter Mary had married Sir David (Davy) Owen, reputedly the natural son of Owen Tudor, grandfather of Henry VII. Before their son Henry was old enough to inherit, his mother died, sometime before 1500.

As well as administering the estate, Sir David was now given a tenancy for life and he exercised his rights rather freely. Around 1520 he demolished the old house and began rebuilding in the new Italianate Style, popularised by Cardinal Wolsey in his great palace of Hampton Court.

The new structure, (now known as The Ruins), was laid out round a courtyard 125 feet from north to south and 100 feet from east to west. He began with the East Range, with the chapel, hall and the kitchen tower; then constructed the north range and the west as far south as the gatehouse.

Recent studies suggest that the demolition was incomplete; the tracery in the chapel window is gothic suggesting a date before 1520, while the base of the kitchen tower may be part of the old building. Some of the present walls are of rubble construction, suggesting that material was reused, but after Sir David's death in 1535 his widow, Anne Devereux, petitioned the king "desyring your grace that I may have delyvered unto me all the hole tymbre, yrone, lede, tyles, breke, and glasse of the howse of Cowthery, which was gevyne hooley to me by my sayd husband, in hys lyfe tyme, to buyld my howse at Bodyngton (Buddington) with that same."

Sir William FitzWilliam

Sir David's son Henry seems to have got into debt, since in 1527, he illegally sold the revision of the estate, to Sir William Fitzwilliam, making him the heir to the property. In 1529 he sold him the estate outright for £2193 6s 8d although his father was allowed to live there for the rest of his life.

Sir William was a prominent courtier, a former ambassador to France, Privy Councillor, Knight of the Garter and Treasurer of the Royal Household. In 1533 he obtained a licence to impark 600 acres of land, meadow, pasture and wood lying in Easebourne and Midhurst "to be called and named the park of Cowdray for ever and to have a free warren and a several fishery therein, and all the rights and privileges belonging thereto". The raised causeway leading across the Town Meadow was probably constructed at this time and the bridge about halfway along may mark the original course of the river, which was later diverted nearer the House (the bridge at the east end of the causeway is 18th century).

At the same time he obtained a licence to crenellate the building; that is provide it with battlements to resemble a castle. He built the great staircase, enlarged the chapel and constructed a porch leading into the hall. This was decorated with carved pomegranates, the symbol of Katherine of Aragon who was currently in disgrace, and he may have been a secret sympathiser. He also completed the west range with its gatehouse, and added the south range. This contained a gallery with paintings of the twelve Apostles, mischieviously known as Raskalls' Row.

Other Tudor work included the Conduit House, the two storey octagonal structure to the north of the main building. The inspiration for this was possibly an erotic book "Hyponerotomachia Poliphili" published in 1499 in Venice and later translated as "The Strife of Love in a Dreame". The upper storey may have been a dining hall, looking out over the park and reached by two external stairways which were later removed. It could also have functioned as a bathhouse and been used to hold water tanks which connected to the House. This supply was mentioned in the caption of map no. IV. Some of the water was piped to a fountain in the centre of the courtyard; this was described as 'the finest example of Renaissance bronze work outside Italy.' For years after the fire, it lay in pieces, before being re-assembled at Woolbeding; then in 1971 it was loaned to the Victoria and Albert Museum for 100 years.

The entire work took only about 20 years. Later owners added bays and windows, but the ruins are essentially those of an early Tudor great house. The fire that almost destroyed the building in 1793 at least meant that it was spared the radical modernisation, which was such a feature of the Victorian period.

In 1536 Sir William was created High Admiral of England, Wales, Ireland, Normandy and Aquitaine. In August of the next year, Henry VIII visited Cowdray and on 18th October, Sir William became the Earl of Southampton. The King paid another visit in July 1538 and three months later Sir William became Lord Privy Seal.

He had one unwilling visitor, his aunt Margaret Pole, Countess of Salisbury, whom he arrested on behalf of the king and imprisoned at Cowdray during the winter of 1538-9. She was the last descendant of the Plantagenants, a staunch Roman Catholic who refused to allow her tenants to read the New Testament, and who was suspected of supporting the rebellion known as the Pilgrimage of Grace in the north of England.

Her son Reginald was a former rector of South Harting, who became a Cardinal. He denounced Henry VIII in the treatise, "De Unitate Ecclesiastica" and encouraged dissent among exiles in the Low Countries. Lady Margaret was later transferred to the Tower of London where she was beheaded in 1541 for treason, despite strenuous attempts to distance herself from her son's views.

Sir Anthony Browne

In 1542 Sir William was commanding an English army which was preparing to attack the Scots, when he died and was buried at Newcastle-on-Tyne. He had no heir, so his estate passed to Sir Anthony Browne, his half brother by his mother's second marriage.

Sir Anthony was knighted for bravery when only 23, and had already held high office including that of Lieutenant of the Isle of Man. In 1533 he attended a conference in Nice with the Pope in a final attempt to annul the King's marriage to Catherine of Aragon, and three years later helped suppress the Pilgrimage of Grace. He stood guard at the christening of Prince Edward, was proxy for Henry in his ill-fated marriage to Anne of Cleves, acted as spokesman for the physicians when warning the king of his impending death, and was guardian to his successor.

In August 1545 a meeting of the Privy Council was held at Cowdray at which the King was probably present. However Sir Anthony spent most of his time at Battle Abbey near Hastings, where he died in 1548. His father had acquired the property following the dissolution of the monasteries, and it remained in family hands until 1719.

The First Viscount

His eldest son, another Sir Anthony inherited his Sussex Estates. He was just 21 and a strong Roman Catholic like his father, but he possessed great diplomatic skills enabling him to work with three Tudor monarchs of widely different religious persuasions. He was probably responsible for laying out the formal gardens, north and east of the main buildings, with a walled privy garden to the south. Three pavilions were also built, one of which still stands next to the river, south of the stables.

In 1551 he was imprisoned for hearing Mass but he soon found favour with the Protestant Edward VI, who visited him at Cowdray. Writing to a friend, the King referred to the 'goodly house of Sir Anthony Browne's where we were marvellously, yea rather excessively bannetted'.

When Mary became Queen in 1553, he became more prominent. On 2nd September 1554 the Queen created him Viscount Montague, 'in consideration of the good and laudable service' on the occasion of her marriage to Philip of Spain. The title Montague was probably chosen since his grandmother Lucy was the daughter and co-heir of the Marquis Montacute. The same year he was made Master of the Horse and sent with Thurby, Bishop of Ely, to the Pope in order to make arrangements 'for reducing of this realm to a union with the Church of Rome and to the obedience of that See.'

He became a Privy Councillor in 1555 and Knight of the Garter and in 1557 acted as Lord Lieutenant of English forces at the siege of St. Quentin in Picardy. However when Elizabeth I became Queen in 1558, he lost his position on the Council.

He faced a serious dilemma two years later when he was one of only two peers to refuse 'out of a sentiment of zeal and honour' to subscribe to the acts of supremacy and uniformity that restored Protestantism. He declared that 'he for his part had, by authority of Parliament, and in the name of the whole body of England, tendered obedience to the Pope; the performance of which he could by no means dispense with… it would be a very disgraceful reflection for England, which was so lately and so well reconciled by the Apostolic See, to make so sudden a revolt from it…'

He was ordered to suppress a chantry he had established in Midhurst church (a chapel where masses were sung for the dead), but despite this, the Queen sent him in 1561 on a special mission to Spain. He had to explain why she had attacked the Scots and of the dangers posed by the French House of Guise if their influence continued unchecked. (Mary of Guise had married the Scottish King James V and their daughter Mary became Queen of Scots).

Elizabeth 'highly esteemed him for his great prudence and wisdom, though earnestly devoted to the Romish religion.' Then in 1565 he was sent on another mission to the Duke of Parma, Spanish Regent of the Low Countries.

In 1570 Pope Pius V issued a bull excommunicating Elizabeth and releasing her subjects from their allegiance to her. (The word bull is derived from the medieval Latin "bulla" meaning seal or sealed document). This had the unfortunate effect of calling into question the loyalty and patriotism of English Roman Catholics, but despite this, in 1587, the Queen gave him another sensitive appointment as one of 47 commissioners at the trial of Mary Queen of Scots.

Next year with the Spanish Armada looming, Elizabeth I viewed her troops at Tilbury Fort. Sir Anthony, although elderly and infirm, was said to be the first nobleman to arrive together with his son and grandson and nearly 200 horsemen. Then in August 1591 he entertained the Queen for nearly a week at Cowdray. Due probably to their religious differences there was no church service on the Sunday, instead there was a breakfast featuring three oxen and 140 geese.

The festivities included speeches of welcome from actors dressed as a porter, a pilgrim, a wild man and an angler and there was an outdoor meal with a table 48 yards long. A hunt was arranged where Elizabeth killed three or four deer penned in a paddock, and she watched while greyhounds pulled down 16 bucks on the lawn. (A herd was kept on the estate until after the Second World War, when due to problems of increased traffic and inadequate fencing it was necessary to dispose of it).

Sir Anthony's eldest son died in June 1592 and he himself only lived till October. He was buried in Midhurst Church with his two wives, but the monument was removed in 1851 and later transferred to Easebourne Church.

The Second Viscount

His grandson, Anthony Maria Browne, was only 20 when he became the Second Viscount, but he was already married to Lady Jane Sackville, daughter of Lord Dorset, the High Treasurer of England. (Feminine names were often given to men in this period).

In 1595, he issued his 'Book of Rules and Orders for the better direction and government of my householde and family, together with the severall dutyes and changes appperteryninge to myne officers and other servants.' This describes the rigid protocol governing the running of the household which included elaborate processions each time a course was served at dinner. Horace Walpole described it as 'a ridiculous piece of mimicry of royal grandeur; and instance of ancient pride… there are no fewer than thirty-six different ranks of servants whom he calls his officers; and yet…no mention is made of his chaplains or priests.'

In practice it would have been unwise to mention them. Under the severe recusancy laws of 1581, he would be subject to a fine or imprisonment for even hearing mass. (A recusant was an individual who refused to attend services of the Church of England).

His greatest crisis occurred following the Gunpowder Plot of 1605 when he was accused of complicity. Thirteen years earlier he had employed Guy Fawkes as a servant although he blamed his grandfather for making the appointment. He was also absent from Parliament on November 5th, claiming that his grandmother had stopped him going since she thought the hard riding would be too much for his health!

He was brought before Star Chamber, fined £4000, and ordered to be detained during the King's pleasure. But he only spent 40 weeks in the Tower, probably escaping a greater punishment due to the intervention of his father-in-law.

A legal case of a different kind arose after a burglary on 5th February 1610. Five men were accused of stealing bed linen, tablecloths, towels and clothes with a total value of £12/8/4. One, Mark Russell, was hanged, two were tried later, a fourth was acquitted, while the fifth remained at large. Three women were charged with being accessories, but there is no record of their trial.

Sir Anthony was always short of money. This was partly due to the penalties he incurred for recusancy, but he was also extravagant, for instance giving two daughters £1500 to buy clothes for a wedding! However he did some remodelling of the House, including putting bays on the Eastern Range and the building plans still exist, the earliest to survive for Cowdray.

In 1625, a holy year for Roman Catholics, Pope Urban VIII wrote to Lord Montague noting that 'of late you have erected in your own house, and fittingly adorned, a private chapel in honour of the Blessed Sacrament and of the Blessed Virgin Mary.... by the advice of Our venerable brethren, the Cardinals of the Holy Roman Church... and of our Apostolic authority... do decree and declare that the aforementioned chapel of the Blessed Sacrament and of the Conception and Assumption into Heaven of the Virgin Mother of God, shall hereafter and forever be held by all to be a sacred place, and be named as it ought to be named Conception and glorious Assumption of the same Blessed Virgin Mary...'

The reason for this licence is unclear; the chapel had been built 100 years earlier so this was likely to be a rededication. It seems unlikely the letter was made public although the pressure on Roman Catholics was easing, King James I had just died and been followed by his son Charles I who had a wife of that persuasion.

A rare devotional book

Other evidence of Roman Catholic devotion was discovered in 1963 during modernisation of a chimney at number 27, Glazier's Lane Easebourne. This was a small book entitled 'The Litle Memorial concerning the good and frvitfvll vse of the Sacraments', published in 1602, and translated from the Spanish original by Father Francis Arias of the Society of Jesus.

This devotional book may well have been hidden by a priest, perhaps during the period of the Commonwealth, when Jesuit missionaries were particularly at risk.

The Third Viscount

Sir Anthony died in 1629 and was succeeded by his son Francis Browne. He was 20 and another staunch Roman Catholic. One of his employees was the French trained chef Robert May, who in 1660 was to publish "The Accomplisht Cook, or the Art and Mystery of Cookery' the most important cookery book of its time.

When the Civil War began, Sir Francis supported King Charles, supplying him with money and arms. In response on 27th June 1643, Parliament resolved 'that the estate of the Lord Viscount Montague, a papist, be forthwith sequestered.'

To begin with Cowdray House was safe, since Sir Ralph Hopton, the Royalist general had garrisoned it, with horses being stabled at the priory. However as a precaution the valuable historical murals were covered in lime wash, though this did not prevent the face of Henry VIII being damaged in an accident.

Then the Parliamentary General Sir William Waller (known informally as William the Conqueror!) advanced from Farnham and on Monday 11th December 1643 'wheeled about towards Medhurst where my Lord Montacute's house is, which said Lord is a known and profest Papist: the house is now possest by the Parliament forces; where we staid that night and furnished the said castle (for indeed it may well be called so in regard of the strength thereof) with all the necessaries for defence to awe the Papists and malignants, whereof the said town is much infested and infected…'

A parliamentary order of 1st April 1644 required that 'Captain Higgons do forwith sent up the plate, treasure, and other goods found in the Lord Montague's House.' These were held for a time in Camden House in Notting Hill, and then on 6th June it was decreed that they should be 'sold. at the best value.' The House was cleared so efficiently that an inventory of 1682 shows it to be bare of all its former riches of renaissance splendour except for some historic paintings, while the Buck's Hall, (so named as it contained 11 life size carvings of bucks) was only being used for domestic purposes. The Second Viscount's Household Rules were probably kept at the Priory and so survived.

But there was a greater threat. On the 28th September 1644 an urgent letter was sent to the parliamentary governor of Chichester. 'We are informed that you intend the demolishing of [Cowdray] House, whereat we cannot but wonder, considering the ill consequences such a demolition would draw upon that country. We therefore desire you to take speedy and effectual order for the stopping of the said demolishing, and to provide that house with such a garrison as you with Colonel Stapley shall think fit for the keeping under of the ill-affected party, which we hear is too great in those parts."

The message arrived just in time; 11 days later, 60 foot soldiers and ten horses were billeted on Cowdray under a person of trust, with victuals and ammunition. Later the detachment was increased to 120 foot soldiers and the troops stayed there till the Restoration in 1660. The family estates continued to produce an annual rent of £1575, but two thirds of this was sequestered by Parliament due to Viscount Montague's recusancy.

Sir Francis was now very short of money. He sold an estate at West Horsley in Surrey and rented out much of the land and buildings at Battle Abbey. Despite this, he was very extravagant, spending £1945/10/- in one year on minor items. Then in 1666 the King imposed a levy of 1% on personal estates and in 1670 a tax of two shillings a year on every hearth in any house worth a pound per year, there were 77 hearths in Cowdray House alone!

He also had domestic sadness. He quarrelled with his eldest son Anthony who went abroad, reaching The Hague at the outbreak of the Civil War. Returning, he married Bridget, daughter of a member of the landed gentry in York, and was wounded in the leg at the siege of that city in 1644. He was imprisoned but then escaped to Derbyshire where he lived under the assumed name of John Hudson.

At the restoration, Bridget failed to regain possession of her father's estates, which Cromwell had confiscated, so Anthony returned to Cowdray to make peace with his father. The new servants did not recognise him, telling him that Sir Francis had gone abroad, so he returned to Derbyshire where he died in 1666.

The Fourth and Fifth Viscounts

Lord Montague died in London in November 1682, and left Cowdray 'in its dilapidated condition.' He was succeeded by his 44-year old son, Francis, who was also very short of money. He demolished the great kitchen at Battle Abbey so he could sell the materials, but destruction of a more natural kind also occurred in the Great Storm of November 1703. It was reported that 'four or five stacks of Chimneys are blown down at my Lord Montacute's House…one of them fell on the Great Hall, which did Considerable Damage… and my Lord had above 500 Trees torn up by the Roots; and… Several Barns blown down…'

His fortunes improved when the Roman Catholic James II ascended the throne. Letters patent were granted to him so that a fortnightly market could be held in Midhurst together with fairs in March, July and October. He was even made Lord Lieutenant of Sussex in January 1688, but this appointment lapsed within a year when the King fled to France.

He had no heir, and in 1689, his nephew Gervase, son of Anthony Browne, approached him with his claim to be Viscount. 'He was duly acknowledged and promised the next succession to the title, when, it was argued, he might have it without trouble or expense.' He duly registered his claim in the Herald's Office, but died seven years later.

Sir Francis lived until 1708. He was succeeded by his brother Henry, who had had the dubious distinction of having being given the title of Secretary of State for England by the exiled James II in 1691. In 1712 he employed Thomas Heather to make a survey of the estate. He died at Epsom in June 1717.

The Sixth Viscount

He was succeeded by his 31-year old son Anthony Browne. Two years later he sold Battle Abbey, which over the years had become very dilapidated and allegedly provided a storehouse for smugglers.

He did a considerable amount of work on the Easebourne estate. This included installing iron gates at the west end of the causeway, (these were moved to their present position in the 1960s). He also built stables by the river, dated 1726 and the 'base court' round a square south of the main house. This contained service facilities including a bake-house, brew-house, malting-house, boulting-house (where flour was sieved) and a stillroom or pantry.

These structures survived the fire of 1793 and in the early 20th century were converted into the 'laundry cottages', while the dairy was decorated with Royal Doulton tiles depicting local scenes. These buildings had been joined to the Kitchen Tower, but a gap was now made to provide access to the Polo grounds.

In 1732 he was chosen as Grand Master of the Freemasons. However six years later Pope Clement XII issued his bull 'In Eminenti' declaring that any of the faithful who joined the fraternity were guilty of grave sin, and were in danger of excommunication.

In 1749 Horace Walpole visited and wrote 'our greatest pleasure was seeing Cowdry which is repairing; Lord Montacute will at last live in it... I was charmed with the front, and the court, and the fountain, but the room called Holbein's, except the curiosity of it, is wretchedly painted, and infinitely inferior to those delightful stories of Harry the VIII, in the private apartments at Windsor...'

Sir Anthony died in 1767 aged 82 and was buried under a raised table-tomb of black marble in the cloister of Easebourne Priory, though this has now been reduced to a floor panel in the south chapel. He seems to have been fortunate, many Roman Catholics were buried without any inscription or record in the church register, since clergymen like Serenus Barrett, the vicar of Midhurst Church, refused to make any entry as to the baptism, marriage or burial of a 'Romanist.'

A Protestant Viscount

The seventh Viscount, Anthony Joseph Browne who was born in 1728, married Frances Mackworth, a dedicated follower of the Countess of Huntington, a famous Protestant evangelist. They had two children, a daughter Elizabeth May born in 1767 and a son George Samuel who was two years younger.

Anthony also became a Protestant and closed the chapel although he did build a meeting place for the local Roman Catholics, the first such structure to be erected in Sussex since the Reformation. After the lease on the Chapel and Priest's house lapsed in 1856, the building became part of the Easebourne Village Institute, and still functions as such.

He was anxious to make improvements to the park and in 1768 engaged Lancelot (Capability) Brown, paying him £3450 over the next six years. Perhaps as a result of this and similar expenditure, in 1781 he mortgaged the estate for £18.000.

Capability Brown removed the formal gardens and replaced the bowers of oaks with clumps of trees. In the process he destroyed a considerable part of the thickets and trees in Close Walks, an area of woodland where Elizabeth I had been entertained. He may also have been responsible for cutting down the elm trees planted along the causeway, but he did spare the avenue of Spanish Chestnuts, said to be the finest in England. He also constructed the ha-ha, (a ditch and sunken wall, preventing animals straying into the gardens, while preserving a vista of open countryside.)

Within the house, Sir Anthony employed Italian artists to decorate the staircase and some of the rooms. He also had a hobby, turning ivory using a lathe, and he filled a cabinet with some 'very neat pieces', many containing small and delicate flowers.

In 1780 there was a visit by Samuel Hieronymus Grimm, a Swiss topographical draftsman. He was employed by Sir William Burrell Bart, an antiquarian and MP for Haslemere to produce drawings and paintings of important venues in Sussex.

As well as making engravings of some pictures, Grimm produced 11 paintings, including three views of the façade, the exterior of the building from four angles, two aspects of the courtyard, and the interior of the chapel and Bucks' Hall. Another unsigned, undated picture of the East Front also exists together with three watercolours by Hendrik de Cort. These illustrations have proved invaluable as a record of the House before the fire.

Two years later Dr. Johnson also visited Cowdray. He commented, 'Sir, I should like to stay here four-and-twenty hours. We see here how our ancestors lived.'

In 1783 Lord and Lady Montague settled in Brussels and he died there in April 1787 although he was buried at Easebourne. On his deathbed, he renounced Protestantism, and reverted to the faith of his ancestors, although some thought this reconversion was due to the fact that 'he was literally besieged and taken by assault by the Roman Catholic clergy.'

The Eighth Viscount

George Samuel was educated at Winchester College and succeeded to the title when he was only 18. Later he became engaged to 'the amiable and accomplished' Miss Coutts, daughter of the banker Thomas Coutts.

He clearly enjoyed foreign travel. In 1786 he was upset when his father stopped him visiting him in Brussels, and in May 1793 he was in Venice from where he returned to Cowdray for his 24th birthday on June 26th. Then he set off again with his friend Charles Sedley Burdett, older brother of a famous MP and reformer, Sir Francis Burdett.

In October they decided to shoot the Falls of the Rhine at Laufenburg, midway between Basle and Schaffhausen. This was so dangerous that the local magistrates refused them permission to try, and Dickenson, an old family servant, even grabbed Lord Montague's collar in an attempt to stop him.

They set off with a dog in a specially built boat, but it capsized in the second cataract and they were drowned in a whirlpool. Lord Montague's body was later recovered and buried at Laufenburg, before being transferred to Brugg, the nearest Protestant town.

The Fire

Meanwhile there was disaster at home. The House was being renovated and a glaziers' and carpenters' shop had been set up in the northwest tower. Higgeson, the foreman, allowed his men a charcoal fire despite the fact that the floor was covered in wood shavings. At eleven p.m. on 24th September 1793 flames were seen shooting out of the windows of the tower. Unfortunately most of the paintings had been taken down and stored in the North Gallery. When this caught fire they were almost all destroyed.

The dowager Lady Montague and her daughter had gone to Brighton while the work was in progress, and only the housekeeper, Mrs. Chambers, the porter and one or two servants were still in the House. There was nothing they could do. A hose and fire buckets had been provided, but these were locked in the Conduit House and the key had been mislaid.

Some of the villagers were woken by the flames and rushed to help. They managed to save a few treasures including the altarpiece from the chapel. They even tried to pull down some of the walls to form a firebreak, but the masonry proved too strong.

The only part of the House untouched was the kitchen tower. Traditionally this structure was separate from the main building since most fires were caused by cooking, but in this case it was the means of its preservation. Later a floor was put in to provide an extra room above the old kitchen, where the tenants dined on the occasion of the half-year audits. The dinner was cooked in the kitchen and hoisted up through an aperture since the 'spiral staircase would not allow of the conveyance of the dinner.'

The Ninth Viscount

On the death of the Eighth Viscount, Joseph Browne, the grandson of Gervase Browne, asserted his claim to be Viscount, but he was old and did not have the resources to collect the necessary proofs.

Instead the title went to Mark Anthony Browne, a descendant of John, brother of the Second Viscount, although he did not inherit the estate. He was 49 and a friar at Fontainebleau. He obtained a papal dispensation to set aside his vows, and on 6th February 1797 married Miss Frances Manby at Little Bursted in Essex. However in November of that year he died without issue and the Montague line became extinct. His body was brought to Midhurst in a gorgeous coffin, on which was a large crucifix of gold. It lay in state at the Angel Inn, and was buried under the Browne monument in Midhurst Church.

Mr and Mrs Poyntz

In 1792 George Samuel had made a will leaving all his property to his sister Elizabeth Mary Browne. On 1st September 1794 she married William Stephen Poyntz, a member of a Berkshire family. The double tragedy of the year before must have stunned her, and instead of trying to rebuild the House, she chose to live in the old keeper's lodge, half a mile to the east, which had just been enlarged and turned into a "cottage ornée.". They had two sons, William Montague Browne Poyntz, born in 1801, and Courtney John Browne Poyntz in 1805. They also had three daughters, Frances Selina, Elizabeth Georgina, and Isabella.

Frances married in 1814 but the next year the rest of the family went on holiday to Bognor. On July 7th, Stephen took his two sons and two friends of his daughters, the Misses Parry, for a sail, (the daughters themselves were left behind with their mother because of disobedience). A sudden squall capsized the boat, and everyone drowned apart from Stephen and the boatman.

Although Elizabeth lived another 15 years, she never recovered from the tragedy. She was buried in a new mortuary chapel in Easebourne Church together with her sons. Stephen lived another ten years, suffering constant pain after a riding accident, and was buried with his family.

After his death, in a bizarre return to medieval practice, Mrs Sargent the owner of East Lavington claimed heriot (a tribute paid to a lord out of the belongings of a tenant who had died). She took his best chattel, a team of four Suffolk Punch carthorses, though these were later redeemed for £200. The agent then drew up a lease lasting 10,000 years to prevent a repetition of the problem

The Earls of Egmont and Viscounts Cowdray

The estate was now divided among the three daughters. The eldest, Frances, wanted to buy out her sisters, but this proved impossible, so in 1843 Cowdray was sold for £330,000 to George James the Sixth Lord Egmont, a distinguished admiral.

He continued to live in the Keeper's Lodge until his death in 1874. He had no heir, so his nephew Charles George inherited the title. Five years later he had the Lodge pulled down, and the present Cowdray House built on the site. He also died childless in 1897, and was succeeded by another relative Augustus Arthur, who again died without issue in 1910. However on 23rd September 1908 he had sold the estate for £340,000 to Sir Weetman Dickson Pearson.

The Pearson Family and S.Pearson & Son.

The Pearson fortune had its origins in a humble 19th Century brick making business in West Yorkshire. Samuel Pearson (Weetmans grandfather) started work as a navvy and progressed to brick making and quarrying. He only learned to read and write late in life but even so he was able to found S. Pearson & Son in 1856, the year Weetman was born. When he died in 1884 he left the then considerable sum of £20,000.

Weetman Dickson Pearson (1856-1927)

Young Weetman left school at 16, by 17 he was in charge of one of the family brick works and by 19 had set sail for South America where the company developed and prospered.

S. Pearson & Son developed into one of the great civil engineering and construction companies of the late Victorian era, building railways in Spain and China, as well as England and Ireland, docks in Southampton, Halifax Nova Scotia and Dover Harbour. They also built the Blackwall Tunnel, the East River Tunnels in New York and opened up the Kent coalfields. In Mexico they built the Grand Canal, drained Mexico City, built railways coast to coast and provided towns with electric light, pure water and modern sanitation. Weetman established the Mexican Eagle Oil Co. in competition with Standard Oil of America, eventually selling out to Shell.

He was created a Baronet in 1894 and in 1905, leased the Cowdray Estate of 17,000 acres with an option to buy from the 8th Earl of Egmont. He purchased it in 1908, abandoning his original plan to build a castle on high ground. Instead he devoted much time and money to the alteration and improvement of the current house and on the repair and preservation of the Priory at Easebourne and the ruin of the old house.

In 1910 he was created Baron Cowdray of Midhurst. In 1914 he lost his youngest son, Geoffrey who was killed in action, while an older son, Clive, was seconded to help him in the oil business. In 1917 he advanced to Viscount and the following year he moved to his estate at Paddockhust, near Turners Hill in East Sussex, and the Dunecht Estate in Aberdeenshire, leaving Cowdray to his eldest son Harold.

Weetman Harold Miller Pearson (1882-1933)

Harold captained the Oxford University polo team in 1905. In 1906-18 he was Liberal MP for the Eye Division of Suffolk and in World War I served as a Major in the Sussex Yeomanry. During this time he married the grand daughter of the 6th Duke of Marlborough by whom he had six children, Yoskyl, John and Angela (twins), Nancy, Benda and Daphne. In 1919 he inherited the Cowdray Estate and became the Second Viscount Cowdray on the death of his father in 1927.

Weetman John Churchill Pearson (1910-1995)

In 1933 Weetman John Churchill Pearson succeeded to the title becoming the Third Viscount Cowdray and inheriting the Cowdray and Dunecht estates. In 1940, as a Captain in the Sussex Yeomanry, he came under heavy fire and his left arm had to be amputated. He is reputed to have said "At least I won't have to play golf again"! He was a parliamentary private secretary to the Under Secretary of State for Air 1941-42, sitting in the House of Lords as a Liberal and from 1950 as an Independent. In 1951 he bought the 805,000 acre Matador Ranch in Texas, the second largest in the USA.

Between 1954 and 1977, he was chairman of S. Pearson & Son, which owned the merchant bankers Lazard Bros, the publishing firms of Pearson, Longman and Penguin, the Financial Times, Economist, Investors Chronicle and the Westminster Press also Royal Doulton and interests in American and North Sea Oil. In 1962 he acquired a controlling interest in Chateau Latour and later added Chessington Zoo and Madam Tussauds.

His one extravagance was Polo, playing fearlessly despite the loss of his arm and he made this an increasingly popular sport. He captained Oxford University and was Chairman of the Hurlingham Polo Association, the games governing body, from 1947 to 1967.

Michael Orlando Weetman Pearson

The Fourth Viscount Cowdray succeeded to the title in 1995 and with the local community and English Heritage set up the Cowdray Heritage Trust.

The Ruins

From 1793 to 1912 the ruins were very largely abandoned, although they became a tourist attraction. Visitors were intrigued by the ivy-covered walls, the clock which had stopped at the moment of the fire, and the story of a doomed family. Many paintings were made, and there were visits by John Constable and J. M. W. Turner.

William Cobbett came to Midhurst in November 1825 on one of his 'rural rides.' He reported 'we entered the park through the great iron-gateway, part of which being wanting, was stopped up by a hurdle. We rode down to the house and all round about and in amongst the ruins, now in part covered with ivy, and inhabited by innumerable starlings and jackdaws.'

An Architectural Antiquary writing in 1834 noted 'the noble ruins of the house are fast hastening to extinction. In windy weather the public are not allowed to approach the walls lest the fall of some tall gable or lofty window should prove fatal to the visitors; and the owner, to avoid a calamity of this kind, caused a tower on the south side, and some other fragments to be demolished.... This is the system adhered to at Cowdray; a fragment that exhibits dangerous decay is pulled down to save its falling at an unlucky moment, and (what is of equal consideration) to save a few pounds which would secure it in its place...'

One casualty was the northwest tower. An early picture of the ruins shows two fragments of the outside wall still standing, but these had gone by 1809. Similarly a view of the hall range in 1859 revealed a whole stack of chimneys and an important fragment that had vanished by 1919. Much of the damage was caused by the 'beautiful but terribly destructive ivy'; photographs taken in 1910 show the ruins shrouded in it.

But it was not only the structure that suffered. A pupil of Midhurst Grammar School also writing in 1834 noted 'at the south end is a massive tower of large dimensions which has escaped the fury of the flames; the kitchen occupies the ground-floor and is nearly filled with faggots and rubbish; by a winding staircase you reach another room of equal dimensions with the kitchen; the floor is covered with ancient deeds, valuable MSS., and private letters which are suffered to lie about in wild confusion, submitted to the inspection of every visitor.'

Much if not most of this archive was destroyed or stolen by casual visitors before Lord Egmont limited access. Our scant knowledge of the early history of the site may well stem from this neglect.

The ruins were used as a cattle yard, but census returns indicate that some people lived there. In 1841 James and Hannah Street aged 50 shared the site with William and Fanny Boxall aged 45 and 35 and their two sons William and Henry aged 15 and 10; Fanny Boxall was still in residence 30 years later. The Conduit House was also used; in 1881 nine people from two families occupied it.

Conservation

Apart from the removal of ivy from the walls in 1881, no conservation work was done until Sir Weetman Dickson Pearson bought the estate. Initially he employed Sir Aston Webb, President of the Royal Academy, to superintend restoration. During the next five years a comprehensive programme was carried out with some work continuing until 1916.

Sir William H St. John Hope joined the project in 1913 and wrote a very detailed description of the history and structure of the House in his book ' Cowdray and Easebourne Priory in the County of Sussex', published after his death in 1919.

The first task was to eradicate all the ivy and bushes growing inside or on the ruins. Then the tops of the walls were made good using clay tiles to prevent the entry of rainwater and loose parts of the structure were stabilised. St. John Hope then supervised the excavation of the destroyed parts of the building and where the walls were removed below ground level. Their lines were shown above ground by building rubble-based walls based upon their foundations. He made no attempt at restoration beyond the necessary replacement of lost mullions and other structured parts.

It is largely due to his efforts that so much of the structure survived the twentieth century. Some of his practices, such as replacing wooden lintels with concrete, have caused problems, but his main work was sound.

Some additional work was done in the 1950s when the porch roof was replaced with concrete and asphalt and another, ten-year programme was initiated in 1975, although it did not achieve all its objectives.

English Heritage did some investigations on the site in 1984 and 1987 and in March 1999 a successful bid was submitted to the Heritage Lottery Fund by the Cowdray Trust, supported by the four local authorities. Work was in progress in 2006 on the Grade I listed structure, with a planned opening date of Easter 2007.

Tudor Gardens

Another important renovation was the Walled Privy Garden. In November 2001 it was a jungle of grass, weeds and brambles. However under a three-year plan devised by garden designer Jan Howard, it was converted back to a medieval design with a modern twist. Together with her husband, a project manager, a landscape gardener and a gardener, the site was levelled and drained, then planted.

When complete, visitors would enjoy arched rose walks, fruit and yew trees, box topiary, herbs, herbacious areas, a fruit cage and vegetables. The plan was to produce something that Queen Elizabeth 1st who came here in 1591 would have recognised.

The Stables

With the development of stables near The Ruins for business purposes, several new firms arrived in the parish at the start of the 21st century. By 2006, these included Restalls (violin makers, restorers and dealers), Fur, Feather & Fin (country sports) and Simplicité (skin care).

Sources
Fowler, Daryl; Harridge, Nicola & Tite, Graham (1999) "A conservation plan for the Cowdray Ruins, Midhurst, Appendix 1, Historical Studies", Broadway Malyan Cultural Heritage.
Roundell, Mrs. Charles (1884) "Cowdray, the History of a Great English House". Bickers and Son.
Salzman L.F. (1953) "The Victoria History of the Counties of England". Volume IV, OUP.
St. John Hope, William H. (1919) "Cowdray and Easebourne Priory", Country Life.
Trotter, Torrens (1922) "Cowdray, Its early history". Cowdray Estate Office.
"United", Church and Parish Magazine, from April 1973 onwards.
"100 years of Golf at Cowdray Park" (1994).
Bone, Dr. Anne. Chichester District Council. (Unpublished).

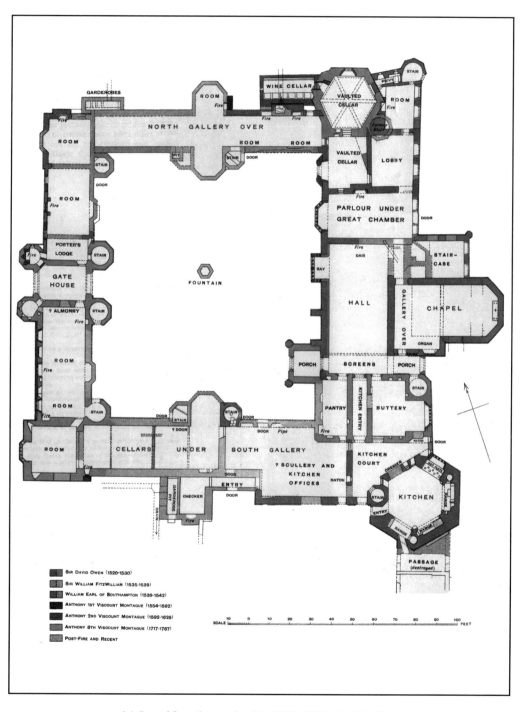

GARDEROBES

ROOM
Fire

WINE CELLAR

PRIVY

STAIR

VAULTED
CELLAR

ROOM
Fire

Fire

ROOM

Fire   Fire

NORTH GALLERY OVER

Former
Stair

STAIR

ROOM   ROOM

DOOR

ROOM

VAULTED
CELLAR

LOBBY

DOOR

STAIR

DOOR

ROOM
Fire

Fire

PARLOUR UNDER
GREAT CHAMBER

DOOR

PORTER'S
LODGE

Fire   STAIR

Fire
DAIS

STAIR-
CASE

GATE
HOUSE

FOUNTAIN

BAY

? ALMONRY

STAIR

Fire

HALL

GALLERY OVER

CHAPEL

+
+

ORGAN

ROOM

Fire

PORCH

SCREENS

PORCH

STAIR

ROOM

Fire

STAIR

PANTRY

KITCHEN
ENTRY

BUTTERY

Fire

HATCH   DOOR

DOOR
STAIR

STAIR   DOOR

DOOR   *Pipe*

ROOM   CELLARS   UNDER   SOUTH GALLERY

KITCHEN
COURT

CRESSET

DRESSER

? DOOR

Fire

GARDEROBE
PIT

CHECKER

Fire

ENTRY

DOOR

DOOR

? SCULLERY AND
KITCHEN
OFFICES

HATCH

KITCHEN

RANGE

DRAIN

STAIR

ENTRY

RANGE   RANGE

PASSAGE
(destroyed)

10   0   10   20   30   40   50   60   70   80   90   100
SCALE   FEET

2.1 Ground floor plan, produced in 1919 by William St. John Hope.

2.2   The Ruins are seen across the parish boundary from Midhurst, before the gates were transplanted from the site of the bus park in the mid-1960s.

2.3   The varied styles of the present Cowdray House are evident in this view of the south elevation. The structure in the foreground is a "Ha Ha".

✃ 3. St Mary's and The Priory ✄

A Centre of Worship

Inevitably any account of the church and priory will focus on the buildings, their history and the people associated with them. But the real significance of this foundation is its function as a centre of worship and the service of God, a rôle it has fulfilled for at least 900 years. This was stressed by Helen Hinkley who dedicated her 1948 guidebook 'in love for the past and hope for the future to all those who in every century have found their spiritual home in this church and shall continue to do so.'

Norman Church

There may have been a minster here in the Saxon period, although no trace remains now. The original Norman building was quite small. Sir William H St. John Hope who surveyed the church in 1913 thought it consisted of a chancel and nave 55 feet long by 18½ wide, with a wooden belfry at the west end. The only part to survive is the south wall and some fragments in the other walls.

Later in the 12th century, a narrow aisle was added to the north, opening out into the nave through three large arches, and a tower was built on the west end. The first spire was blown down in the great gale of 1703. In between 1291 and 1535 the chapels of Midhurst, Fernhurst, Lodsworth and Todham were attached to it, supporting the priory. Todham Church, which was built on the other side of the Rother was later destroyed and after West Lavington Church was built, the parishioners were transferred there in 1851.

Priory

Around the year 1055 Robert de Montgomery refounded Séez Abbey in Normandy. After the conquest, William granted him extensive lands in Sussex, and he made over the income of several local churches to support this foundation. Easebourne may have been among these, and certainly in the early 12th century Savaric fitz Cana, the Lord of the Manor, bestowed the church on the abbey. Later this gift must have been revoked, perhaps after King John lost Normandy, and when Easebourne Priory was founded around 1244, (probably by Sir Frank Bohun), both the church and the chapel at Midhurst were given to endow it.

The priory was dedicated to the Nativity of the Blessed Virgin Mary and accommodated a prioress and ten nuns originally of the Benedictine order, although the house later became Augustinian. It seems to have been a refuge for women from important families, for instance in the late 13th century, one Archbishop requested accommodation for Lucy, daughter of a deceased knight.

The nuns' arrival led to massive structural changes to the church since they appropriated most of the existing building. The chancel became a presbytery for the use of the clergy, while much of the nave became the nuns' quire (or choir) and a wooden belfry was provided for them.

These sections were walled off from the rest of the building, which became the new parish church. Although this included the western half of the old nave and the area under the tower, space was very limited, so the aisle was widened to 21 feet.

North elevation before rebuilding.

3.1   A 1919 photograph shows most of the east elevation, but not the northern part, now used as the vicarage.

(top right)
3.2   The   unusual,   but impressive, interior was recorded at Easter 2006. The former chapel area is on the right and the altar is behind the Revd. Derek Welsman.

(right)
3.3   The bell tower (left) is one of the oldest parts of this historic complex. Part of the east wing (centre) serves as the vicarage and the Refectory (right) is used for a variety of social functions. The foreground is a private area and the wall is all that remains of the "West Range". The wall is reported as 13th century.

Cloister and East Range

A cloister was provided for the nuns in accordance with their rule. This was 85 feet square, situated on the south side of the church. This space is now a garden but originally it was surrounded by a covered alleyway. It is still possible to see where the roof was attached to the east wall, 15 feet above the ground.

A building two stories high was erected on the east side of the cloisters 131 feet long and 28 wide, butting on the new presbytery at its north end. This "range" still exists but the interior has undergone considerable modification and there is some uncertainty about the original arrangement.

There appears to have been a vestry on the ground floor to the north, with a parlour next to it where talking was permitted. The nuns entered the cloisters through a door now obscured by an external staircase, and then processed through the south door of the church into their quire.

South of the old parlour is an eastwards extension, increasing the width of the range to 43½ feet. This extra space accommodated a staircase to the first floor, and the east end of the Chapter House where the business of the priory was conducted. This latter room was a vaulted chamber 23 feet by 38, with three arches on the west end next to the cloister. South of this there was the Warming or Common House, a single room with pillars down the middle. On the upper floor was the Dorter or dormitory. Originally this was 125½ feet long by 22½ wide, partitioned to provide a central corridor with cubicles opening off it. It provided ample space for ten nuns and some novices, though the prioress probably had her own room.

On this level too there was an antechamber in which records, valuables and household linen were stored. There was also another eastwards extension on the south end of the building that housed the Reredortor or latrine. This was later demolished but traces of the drain have been found.

Southern and Western Ranges

There is another two-storied range on the south side of the cloisters. On the ground floor were two rooms both 21½ wide, one 13 feet long and the other 44 feet. These were probably storerooms or cellars.

On the first floor was the Frater or refectory which was nearly 60 feet long. This was accessed by a stairway from the cloisters through an arch, which can still be seen in the north wall. At the east end was a dais where the high table stood and Queen Elizabeth I was later feasted. Food was served from the southeast corner, although no trace of the kitchen has been found. There was also a doorway at the northeast to a room since demolished.

The Western range has disappeared apart from a wall with two doorways. By analogy with other priories, this was probably another two-storied building, supervised by the cellaress, the nun responsible for provisions and catering. On the first floor would be lodging for guests and a parlour below where they were entertained by the nuns. No traces of the gatehouse, infirmary, bake house, brew house or stables have survived.

Endowments

Details of the first endowments are lost, but the priory must have been amply provided for. In 1292 the church and associated chapel at Midhurst were valued at £26/13/4 with temporalities (secular possessions) of £41 and £2 of additional rents. By 1342, there were three more endowments, but the temporalities had fallen to £26/3/8, although it still received the same income from the church and chapel.

In 1409 the advowsons (the patronages) of Compton and Upmarden churches were transferred to Easebourne but three years later the Bishop of Chichester received a report stating 'that on account of epidemics, the deaths of men and servants, and the sterility of the lands of the priory, which is situated in a solitary waste and thorny place; on account of the houses and buildings of the said priory being fallen into ruin and consumed, and of the seizure and loss of rents and revenues which are kept back by certain sons of iniquity; and because the lands and tenements of the prioress and convent notoriously suffer so great ruin that few tenants can be found willing and able to occupy them in these days, and the said lands falling into a worse state, they are so poor that they cannot supply the religious women with sufficient support for themselves and for the repair of their ruinous buildings, etc. now or for the future it is feared.'

In 1414, King Henry V excused the prioress and convent from many taxes for a period of 20 years. Henry VI extended this for three more years; then made the exemption perpetual. The priory may well have been suffering the long-term effects of the Black Death, but there was also evidence of mismanagement.

The Bishop's Visits

Five times between 1402 and 1524 there was an Episcopal Visitation. The Bishop or his deputy, visited the Priory to examine its affairs and interview the personnel, then he made a record of his findings and issued injunctions.

In January 1441 Bishop Richard Praty sent Master Walter Eston his commissionary to Easebourne. He found that the House was £40 in debt largely due to the extravagance of the prioress, 'She frequently rides abroad, and pretends that she does so on the common business of the house, although it is not so, with a train of attendants much too large, and tarries long abroad, and she feasts sumptuously both, when abroad and at home, and is very choice in her dress, so much so that the fur trimmings of her mantle are worth 100 shillings... Also the prioress compels her sisters to work continually like hired workwomen and they receive nothing whatever for their own use from their work, but the prioress takes the whole profit.'

The secular affairs of the house were immediately placed under the control of two men, Thomas Boleyn and John Lylis, until the priory was back in profit. The nuns were allowed to keep half of what they earned, the rest going to pay off the debt. Messrs Boleyn and Lylis supervised the reduction of the prioress' household, and reviewed the hospitality she gave and her journeys outside the priory. She was also ordered to sell her fur, (worth almost one fifth of the yearly income of the church), and pay this into the accounts.

The 1450 Inventory

The priory may have become notorious since when Reginald Peacock became Bishop in 1450, he immediately ordered an inventory. As described by St. John Hope, the priory church was well supplied with service books, and there was also a French Bible, a great legend (lives of the saints), two porthoses (portable prayer-books), and a martiloge (the rule of St Bridget, a Swedish Augustinian nun). These were all handwritten, since the first printed books were only just being produced in Germany.

There were four sets of vestments for the officiating priest, (one red and three cloth of gold) together with two chalices, eight towels and a cross of silver. However bedding was in short supply, there were just two hanging beds, eight other beds with mattresses, eight pillows and twelve pairs of sheets and cushions. Other household items included two dorsers (chair-back covers), three wiping towels and six savenaps (material placed over a tablecloth to protect it from spills).

Food preparation was well provided for, as would be expected given the lavish hospitality for which the house was famous. There were two silver saltcellars, seven basins and 20 candlesticks, while the kitchen boasted four spits, six brass pots, four mortars, four dishes, three cauldrons and 36 garnished vessels. The bake house had an oven with a copper bottom, two flour sieves and two mash tubs. These latter were used to brew beer, the usual beverage before tea and coffee became available.

Livestock included a horse, nine oxen and twenty cows, a bull, 200 sheep, 60 lambs, 40 pigs, two boars, four sows and 20 piglets. Equipment included ploughs, two wagons, a cart and harvesting equipment. The yearly revenue was given as £28/6/8, though the items listed actually amounted to £31/13/4. From this, £6/13/4 was paid to the Vicar and the rest was used to repair the houses. But despite the best efforts of Thomas Boleyn, the debt had now risen to £66/6/8.

For a time the future of the priory was in doubt. It was suggested it should be included in a list of small religious houses that had been suppressed so that the revenue could be given to Bishop William Waynflete for the foundation of his new college of Mary Magdalen at Oxford. But although the priory survived this threat, a cloud of scandal was gathering.

The 1478 Visitation

Less than four months after becoming Bishop of Chichester, Edward Story summoned the Prioress, Agnes Tanke, to his private chapel. She had influential relatives and this was a matter that had to be handled carefully.

It is recorded that "neither compelled by force, or induced by fraud, of her own accord, took her corporal oath... that she would purely, spontaneously, simply and absolutely, without any subsequent delay, resign her office of Prioress, whenever she should be so required by the same Lord Bishop... or... any other person having his authority." She also promised "as soon as possible...to remove and separate the Sub-

Prioress from her office... and that every week, beginning with the eldest, except the aforesaid Sub-Prioress, she should select... one of her nuns as chaplainess for divine services, and to wait upon herself." She also agreed that "neither the Prioress nor any nun should pass out beyond the enclosures of the priory, nor meet together for the purpose of drinking or practising any other improprieties."

Five weeks later, on Saturday June 29th the bishop visited the priory personally and interviewed each inmate in turn without anyone else present. He began with Agnes Tanke.

Apostate Nuns

She reported that two nuns, Joanna Potismouth and Philippa King, "were not of good conversation or disposition, who had withdrawn from the said priory for their health without licence and so are abroad in apostasy at present, but in what place she knows not."

Lady Matilda Astom when asked whether all the services were observed explained that the previous bishop, John Arundel, had excused them the 4 a.m. office. She also said "that certain persons, named John Smyth, chaplain, and N. Style, bond-servant to the Lord Arundel had, and were accustomed to have great familiarity within the said priory, as well as elsewhere, with the said Lady Johanna Potismouth and Philippa King... but whether the said Sir John Smyth and N Style abducted... the said Johanna Potismouth and Philippa King she knows not... and moreover she says that certain William Gosden and John Capron of Easebourne aforesaid, guarded and kept in their own homes the said Johanna and Philippa for some time before their departure from the said priory and...were great encouragers to them in that particular. Also she says that the prioress is very negligent... in the punishment of her delinquent sisters ... moreover... they do not keep silence at the suitable times as they should."

The next two nuns, Lady Johanna Crackelynge and Lady Johanna Steyn, confirmed these accounts and recounted some scurrilous scandal regarding the prioress and the absent nuns. Finally Lady Margaret Lightnore accused a certain Sir John Senoke of spending every night in the priory and of being the ruin of Sir John Smyth. She accused the prioress of giving frequent banquets to her relatives while the nuns made do with much poorer food and of having pledged the House's jewels for £15 to gain a Bull of Capacity for a certain Brother William Cotnall.

This church document entitled him to certain unspecified privileges, although he had defied the prioress by giving Sir John Smyth immunity in any legal action concerning the jewels! He also admitted giving Johanna Potismouth licence to leave the priory and having had carnal knowledge of Philippa King before she left. He also accused the prioress of pledging jewels worth £10 with Sir John Smyth and then forfeiting them.

It is not clear what Bishop Story made of these conflicting accounts or indeed what action he took. The priory itself was in serious financial difficulties, and was exempted in 1485 and 1489 from paying subsidies normally raised from the clergy.

The 1521 Visitation

The next visitation was in August 1521. Bishop Robert Sherburn ordered it, but since he was about 80 years old, he sent a deputy, Master John Worthiall. He was ordered to examine all the nuns under oath, and to require the prioress, Margaret Sackville, to provide a full report on the state of the priory and an inventory. She also had to give an account, year by year, of her administration up to Michaelmas (29th September) 1520, and not to make any changes to the House before the examination.

He began with Margaret Sackville herself, who claimed that the nuns lived honestly and religiously according to the Augustinian rule and were sufficiently obedient to her. Lady Alicia Hill, the sacristan, noted that the cloister roof leaked in the south and west, though the prioress was responsible for buying all the materials necessary to repair it. She was supposed to give each nun 13/4 per annum for clothing, but had failed to do so, or provide an annual report. Three other nuns confirmed they had not received their clothes allowance, and that although the prioress had adequate funds, building repairs had not been carried out.

The prioress was ordered to provide the documentation by October 17th; to make the necessary repairs to the building and give the nuns what was owed them. She was also ordered to provide shutters for the windows of the Nuns' chapel in their living quarters, to provide privacy.

The 1524 Visitation

`Bishop Sherburn ordered John Worthiall to make another visit in 1524. Apart from three new novices, the personnel were the same. When questioned, Margaret Sackville claimed that the priory had made four grants to individuals, but the sub-prioress Lady Alicia Hill, remembered another made to a William Pratt.

Twelve years earlier he was suspected of getting a nun pregnant and he still had "much access to the said priory". She also complained that the novices were insubordinate to her in the absence of the prioress, and that the latter did not present her annual accounts. In reply, several nuns complained that Alicia Hill was too haughty and intolerant, though they confirmed the absence of accounts. They also reported irregularities in the time that matins was sung.

John Worthial ordered the prioress to hold this office each morning at 6 a.m. or 7 a.m. in winter, and keep the door leading into the cloister locked, to prevent unauthorised access to the nuns' quarters. She also had to "render her accounts annually before the convent on pain of deprivation". The sub prioress was ordered to behave well and religiously towards the others, and he gave her a suspended penance.

Sir David Owen's Will and Dissolution.

Sir David Owen who had built much of Cowdray House made his will in 1529. He arranged for a gallery to be built in the Nun's quire connected by a passage and doorway to the dorter, so that the sisters could enter the church without being seen or needing to go downstairs. It would also reduce the risk of unauthorised people entering their living quarters by the door into the cloisters. The ground floor part of their quire was to be returned to the parish church but it would be partitioned off from the presbytery to prevent anyone approaching the altar.

Sir David died in 1535, but it is unlikely that his plans were carried out, since in that year the priory was dissolved. In 1536 all remaining small monasteries were suppressed, the action being justified in the preamble to the legislation. "Forasmuch as manifest synne, vicious carnal, and abominable living, is dayly used and committed commonly in such little and small abbeys, priories and other religious houses... whereby the governors of such religious houses and their convent, spoyle, destroye, consume and utterly waste... to the high displeasure of Almighty God, slander of good religion, and to the great infamy of the King's Highness and realm..." As far as Easebourne Priory was concerned, they may have had a point!

Sir David wished to be buried in the priory church in a brick vault, with effigies of himself and his first wife in new gilt and painted, surrounded by an iron grating. Instead the effigy was placed in an alcove in the north wall while that of his wife has vanished. But one former incumbent of the priory was not forgotten, Baldwin Hammet continued to enjoy a pension of £5 per annum for the next 20 years.

Possessions and Revenues of Priory in 1536 at the time of the dissolution "The Valor Ecclesiasticus"

Compton: farm of rectory etc	£10/0/0
Easebourne with its chapels of Midhurst, Farnhurst, Lodsworth	
and Tadham profits with tithes etc...	£14/8/4
Profits of demesne (estate) lands	£5/0/0
Easebourne: rents	£6/2/3
Worthing: rents	£3/2/0
Chichester: rents	2/6
Greve rent of meadow called Orfford	7/3
Midhurst: rents of lands and tenements	£3/18/0
Farnhurst(Fernhurst) rent of lands	6/8
Sturminster Marshall: rents etc.	£3/0/0

Total	£46/7/0
Less Sinodals (money paid by clergy to bishop); pension (including	
£6/13/4 to Vicar of Easebourne); remission of rent; fees etc	£17/6/5

Total clear value	£29/0/7

New owners

On July 20th 1536, Henry VIII by letters patent (an open document) granted to Sir William FitzWilliam the site with all the buildings of the priory and church, together with the manor of Worthing, and all the other possessions including jewels and ornaments formerly held by Margaret Sackville, at a rent of £23/12/10½. He had previously only enjoyed a peppercorn rent for the priory of one pound of cumin, worth 3d, but now had an income of £29/6/7.

When he died in 1542, the estate passed to his half brother, Sir Anthony Browne and then to his son, another Sir Anthony, the first Viscount Montague.

The priory buildings, apart perhaps for the West Range, were not demolished. In 1591 when Queen Elizabeth I visited Cowdray, 'hir majesty wente to dinner to the Priory where my Lorde himselfe kept house; and there was shee and hir Lordes most bountifully feasted.'

A drawing made by Samuel Hieronymus Grimm in 1780 shows that the Frater floor had been removed, and a large door made in the south wall so the building could be used as a barn. In the early 19th century, the dais end of the Frater where the Queen had dined was converted into a pigeon house. A partition was built and this new room was lined with brick nesting places; some of which still exist.

Another casualty was the nuns' church. After the suppression of the priory, it was dismantled and the roof was removed, leaving it open to the sky.

Burials

Most of the Viscounts Montague were buried in the Easebourne or Midhurst Churches. In 1831, William Poyntz re-roofed the old presbytery to form a memorial chapel for his wife Elizabeth Browne, the Montague family heiress who had died the previous December. He also remembered their two young sons. William Montague aged fourteen and Courtney John aged nine who drowned at Bognor in 1815. When he passed away in 1840, his three daughters placed another monument for him and the chapel also contained the tomb of Anthony the sixth Viscount Montague who had died in 1767 together with his wife Barbara.

In 1851, the tomb of the first Viscount Montague was removed from Midhurst Parish Church, and after being left in a builder's yard for two years, was installed in the chapel. Since space was limited it was drastically modified, the stone obelisks that had stood at either end, were jettisoned and the effigies of his two wives, Jane and Magdalen, were placed side by side.

Workhouse Chaplain

John Serres served Easebourne between 1823 and 1863 and was notable for his work in the Union Workhouse. He became chaplain in 1835 at a stipend of £40, and set up a library for the paupers and supervised the schoolmaster. In 1847 he was commended "for being very zealous in the manner he has carried out the requirements of the committee as regards the moral improvement of women who are classed as the mothers of illegitimate children".

His son followed him in 1848. The new chaplain suggested that a full-time clergyman was needed to deal with female delinquency and he resigned after only two years leaving his father to continue for another seven. Other clergy were less conscientious and had to be reminded by the workhouse committee "that it would be highly advantageous and beneficial to visit this house with a view to the spiritual benefit of their own parishioners who may be inmates."

Rebuilding the church.

Another vicar, Edward Tufnell was involved in two momentous events in the parish. On 30th September 1872 he presided over the first meeting of School Managers (now known as Governors) of Easebourne Schools. They opened on 10th January 1873 and he continued to play an active role until his death six years later.

Then on Saturday 23rd October 1875 there was a meeting to discuss a proposal by the young, seventh Earl of Egmont, current owner of the Cowdray Estate for enlarging and restoring the church. He declared that he was "prepared to undertake the entire cost of the work, leaving farmers or others in the parish at liberty to cart materials for the work if they wish."

He chose a top architect, Sir Arthur Bloomfield, who had once hired the author Thomas Hardy as a gothic draftsman. Sir Arthur worked on the Cathedrals of Salisbury, Canterbury, Lincoln and Chichester, and designed Church House Westminster, Selwyn College Cambridge, an altar in Calcutta and the wooden cathedral of St. George in Georgetown, Guyana.

A plan of the church as it then existed is shown. The old priory church was still separated from the "L" shaped parish church, and the Nuns' quire was open to the sky. There was Horsham stone on the roof, an extra turret and a covered walkway.

They decided to out all present pews and fittings, take up floors and pavements, to remove the present vestry, to take off the roofs and to take down such walls as will be affected by the works hereinafter mentioned. To dig out foundations for all new walls, to erect a new vestry and organ chamber and chancel with local stone and a Bath Stone dressing at the east end of the church, to repair the church throughout with oak open benches (the floor being raised above its present level and a heating chamber for the efficient warming of the church being provided and generally to complete the said church and the repairs and restorations thereof in a substantial and workmanlike manner in accordance with certain plans and specifications which have been submitted to and approved by the Lord Bishop of Chichester."

The memorial chapel was also rearranged, with the Poyntz monuments being shifted to the south wall, the first Viscount's tomb being placed on the east wall and the sixth Viscount's monument next to the chancel. In 1920 with the permission of a Montague descendant, the Marquis of Exeter, this latter was reduced to a slab on the floor, currently obscured by the back row of the choir stalls).

Faculties

In January 1876 the churchwardens paid £11/19/5 to Robert George Raper, the Acting Registrar, for his services in obtaining a faculty from the Bishop of Chichester to allow these alterations. This bill included 6/8 for attending on the Bishop and £1/1/- for chaise hire and expenses!

In view of the scale of these changes, it was necessary to post a bond for £500 in case the work was not completed properly, and in March the vicar paid an additional £1/1/- to license the school building for Divine Service while the church was out of action. Since the school was yet to be extended, it must have been a tight squeeze!

On February 12th Lord Egmont called a public meeting at the School to decide 'whether the sittings in the Restored Church should be Free or Appropriated.' Then on 19th and 20th March, the children received one and a half days' holiday to celebrate the consecration of the church. The licence fees for this procedure cost the parish another £12/11/-.

Reredos

Lord Egmont was in his early 50s when he died in September 1897. In November 1898 a faculty was sought to erect a reredos in his memory. This is a carved screen, which is placed behind the altar; in this case it was again designed by Sir Arthur Bloomfield, and depicted the Last Supper.

Lord Egmont had been a great benefactor of both the school and church and the £400 need to pay for this memorial was raised by voluntary donations. His widow Lucy wrote "It is so kind of the Parishioners of Easebourne to wish to put up a memorial to my dear husband, and I think a reredos would be very nice... he was always saying he should put up one himself, so you could not suggest anything I should like better."

Thwarted plans

In 1914 Sir Weetman Pearson proposed making radical changes to the church including lengthening both the chancel and chapel eastwards and laying a new marble floor. The chancel would be completely refurnished, the organ be enlarged and the tomb of the first Viscount Montague moved and restored to its original condition.

There would also be choir and clergy vestries to replace one demolished in 1876, the choir was currently obliged to robe behind the organ. The tower would be repaired and strengthened, the bells would be rehung and more be added, there would be a new heating system and the churchyard would be extended.

Due to the outbreak of the First World War, these proposals were abandoned or postponed except for the churchyard extension. The new section, which reached westward to the road, was consecrated in June 1915. There was also a new lychgate and a year later a pathway was opened up to the north door of the church after some graves were rearranged.

After hostilities ended, a war shrine was erected in the chapel commemorating the fallen, and an obelisk in the churchyard designed by Sir Aston Webb, president of the Royal Academy. In 1924 he designed a new vestry at the west end and this was built at the same time that the tower was repaired. This had been damaged by vibration caused by bell ringing; so a girder was inserted to strengthen the masonry and a new metal frame installed. This was capable of hanging eight bells; three were added at this time and two more in 1945 in thanksgiving for victory in the Second World War. This completed the peel of eight bells.

Electric light was installed in 1930. Although this might seem a mundane matter, the Bishop's representative Kenneth Mead asked that a message be passed to the parishioners " I am especially grateful with their proceedings and the evident care and thought expended on this."

Treasure and security

There is little further information about the church until 1973 when the parish magazine "United" was launched. Early issues contained two contrasting stories of locksmiths. In 1975 it took 50 minutes and the use of paint strippers and a crowbar to open a locked safe in the refectory. However the eagerly awaited contents only consisted of an empty bottle and a wooden bottle rack!

Two years later there were several thefts from the church. The Bishop's Chair and six vases were taken although two of these were later recovered and the insurance was paid in full. A fund was established to improve security and after taking professional advice, better locks were fitted, and three chests and the new Bishop's Chair were fixed to the floor. Later a second-hand safe was obtained to hold the candlesticks while surplus valuables were sold to boost church funds.

The 1983 Quinquennial Report

The structure of the church is inspected every five years, (the quinquennial report), but there were disturbing findings in 1983. There was extensive Death Watch Beetle infestation; the floor, laid in 1876, had to be renewed immediately and several pews and choir stalls had been affected. Further examination showed that there was also woodworm and dry rot.

The church was out of action for several weeks, with services being held in the Refectory. The floor was finished in time for Christmas, and cost about £11,000. The choir stalls were renewed and 18 interlocking chairs were bought which could be used for small congregations. The opportunity was also taken to change the layout of the church with a freestanding oak altar below the choir and a gold-carpeted sanctuary

The Bishop of Horsham celebrated the completion of the first stage of the work on Easter Sunday, but it was now necessary to redecorate the walls and rewire the building. In the process woodworm and wet rot was found in the roof, and the shingles on the tower needed replacement. It was also necessary to replaster the Montague chapel because of damp.

In all the "Friends of St. Mary, Easebourne" as the restoration fund was now called, spent £21,000 in two years, but assistance was also given by the "Sussex Historic Churches Trust". A carpet was donated which covered the area from the podium to the high altar, and by July 1987 everything had been paid for. The next Quinquennial Report in June 1988 stated that "the church is particularly well cared for, bright and welcoming appearance when entered and those responsible for its day to day care and maintenance are to be congratulated…"

Organ

The organ was built by Henry Bevington and Sons of Soho, in 1876, but when it was restored in 1928, the old fashioned mechanical action was replaced by a tubular pneumatic system. In 1971 a memorial fund for the former organist and choirmaster Reginald William Swanborough raised £1000 and the organ was overhauled and modified. But in 1983 fresh problems emerged.

There was Death Watch Beetle damage and, more seriously; the pneumatic system was close to collapse. When "Songs of Praise" was filmed that year, the BBC employed an organ builder to stand by in case of emergencies, and later at a carol concert, the organist, John Broadbent, had to play with one hand, while pushing in stops with the other!

Initial estimates for repair were about £20,000, and within a year over £13,000 had been subscribed. Then in 1985 a more grandiose plan was announced, the original mechanical action would be restored and the instrument enlarged at a cost of £40,000 by a firm from County Wicklow.

By February 1986, the organ fund stood at £18,000 with a target of £45,000, although an interest free loan of £30,000 had been offered. But then in the summer, the project was reviewed and it was decided to go for a simpler option.

In 1987 the organ was rebuilt and converted to electrical operation by the English organ builder Saxon Aldred, .at a cost of £22,000. As John Broadbent reported "tonally it is now as it was intended, I find it a very exciting instrument to play in many ways.'

Refectory

In 1912 restoration began on the priory. The breach made for the barn doors was filled in, and once more the refectory had two storeys with a new floor and staircase, and a heating system was installed. The hall was furnished with oak chairs and tables, a grand piano and a refectory table similar to those used by the nuns, while Lady Cowdray provided cupboards, sinks, china, and the facilities for making teas. The Chancellor of the Diocese dedicated the building "to the Glory of God and the use of the Easebourne Parishioners" on 25th July 1914.

It may have been at this time that three ponds near the Priory were filled in. They were fed by the stream, and supplied the priory with fish for Fridays and fast days. One villager remembered seeing people skating there in winter or a boy would break up the ice by leading three carthorses across it, so that the pieces could be carted to the icehouse on the side of St. Ann's Hill. The water was originally piped to the old Cowdray House, via the Conduit House, the octagonal building which still stands to the north of it.

Initially the main beneficiary of the Refectory was the school. By November 1917, it was used for cookery lessons, and midday meals. At the beginning of the Second World War the Women's Voluntary Service established a canteen there and this continued into the post-war period. In 1950 there was a serious fire.

Meals cost 5d, and were available for any children in the area. A former pupil remembers boys making unauthorised exits through a hole in the wall by jumping onto the roof of an outside toilet below!

For many years the parish lacked the means to keep the building in proper condition, but in 1973 the ground floor was cleared out and decorated for use as committee rooms. The larger one was renamed in memory of George West, a former churchwarden who had been the superintendent at Budgenor Lodge.

At the same time a new oil-fired heating system was installed using volunteer labour and the building was rewired. That autumn 100 people enjoyed a harvest supper in the hall for the first time in many years.

The parish council were less fortunate. While using the George West Room they complained of noise from the scouts and guides in the hall above and fumes from a "blow-back" by the boiler. The latter problem was solved with the purchase of a gas heater while the young people soon had their own hut, though they were replaced with a badminton club!

In 1987 as the church restoration was almost complete, fresh attention was paid to the Refectory. A new kitchen was installed upstairs, courtesy of the "Tile House" in Easebourne Lane while improvements were made to the downstairs facilities. Then to meet modern fire standards, a second staircase was provided for the hall with assistance from the Parish Council.

The Refectory had been Cowdray property, with the estate being responsible for outside repairs and contributing £100 annually towards running costs. But on 21st October 1988, Lord and Lady Cowdray visited it to present a Deed of Gift of the property to the Vicar and Churchwardens.

The George West room had been extended and was now carpeted. In 1992 the heating system was converted to gas, and six years later, a proper toilet block was installed. Eighty-four years after the Refectory had been designated as a Parish Room it had become an excellent venue for meetings and private functions.

Women's Ministry

Easebourne also played a part in the development in Women's Ministry in the diocese. In January 1988, Sarah Chapman, a reader from Rogate, joined the parish for three months as part of her training to become a deacon. She was 32, married with two young children and was working part time as an occupational therapist at Graylingwell Hospital.

She became a deacon in July 1987 and rejoined Easebourne as a non-stipendiary (unpaid) priest in April 1994. On 4th March 1995 she became the first woman in 900 years to celebrate the Eucharist in

Chichester Cathedral. She told families with young children that they should be free to make as much noise as they liked, she would just lift her voice above theirs!

The event is remembered in a plaque on the wall of Easebourne Church. She left in April 1996 and a year later became Vicar of St. Mary Magdalen, Sheet in Hampshire. However in 2000 she returned briefly to lead an Advent Retreat.

After serving as a deacon at St. Mary's, local resident The Revd. Alison Halliwell MA was ordained into the Priesthood at St. Mary's on 2nd July 2006. This was the first ordination to be conducted in the church and she became its first female priest, although not its vicar. The diocese would still not authorise female ordination in its cathedral.

Millennium

In the autumn of 1998 there were discussions about the best way to celebrate the millennium and it was decided to commission a new stained glass window for the church. But it took a year to get final approval from the Diocesan Advisory Committee, so fund raising could begin.

The design was by Rosalyn Sprey with assistance from Opus Stained Glass of Poynings. As the church is dedicated to the Virgin Mary, she was portrayed at the top holding the Baby Jesus, and below her were the church buildings, the priory and the village. The Es, the stream which gives its name to the parish, was represented by a blue band with bubbles.

The final cost was nearly £5300 and Bishop Lindsay of Horsham dedicated it on 3rd September 2000, a fitting start to the next thousand years.

Fire

Near disaster came with a fire in the choir vestry on 20th December 2006. Thankfully, by chance, one of the ladies involved with arranging the flowers for Christmas needed to go into the vestry, found smoke and allerted the Fire Brigade who came in full force, arresting what could have caused major loss had the fire spread into the body of the church.

Sources

Blaauw, W. H. (1855) **Episcopal visitations of the Benedictine Nunnery of Easebourne**. Sussex Archeological Collections.

Field, Margaret Cary (1977) **Easebourne Priory Church Guide** (Revised)

Gayford, Barbara and others. **United** Church and Parish Magazine, from April 1973 onwards.

Hinkley, Helen E. (1948) **Easebourne - its Church and Priory Guide**

Magilton John & Thomas Spencer (2001) **Midhurst**. Chichester District Archaelogy Vol 1, Chichester District Council

St. John Hope, William H. (1919) **Cowdray and Easebourne Priory**, Country Life.

Partial list of Vicars of Easebourne, (note some of these were classified as Perpetual Curates)

1276 Peter de Wynton
1401 John Bynbrok
1401 Nicolas Coteler
1403 John Byrd
1411 William Hycchecok
1438-9 William Skynnere
1443 Henry Wellys
1444 Thomas Dalby
1485 Richard Skelton
1485 Thomas Wadyngton
1500-1 Robert Milhershe
1510 James Carwardyn

1532 William Ostre
1532 Lancelot Crewe
1649 John Peele
1662 Jefrey Oldfield
1717 Everard Levitt
1749-8 Robert Robson
1751 Francis Atkins
1779 Walter Islip
1813 Samuel Arnott
1823 John Edmund Dominick Serres
1863 Edward Tufnell
1879 Henry Wood

1892 Joseph King Cummin
1912 Charles Edward Hoyle
1935 Thomas Bekenn Avening Saunders
1936 Charles Henry Barker
1944 Richard Paul Peters
1955 Albert William Harrison Harlow
1962 Bernard Robinson Beasley
1972 Clements Hartley Bird
1975 Richard Mark Sweet-Escott
1979 David Burton Evans
1986 Edward Montague Youens
1989 Michael Charles Judge
2002 Derek Brian Welsman

Partial list of Prioresses

1279 Alicia
1302 Isabel de Montford
1313 Edith
1327 Beatrice

1339 Maria
1362 Margaret Wyvile
1411 Margery
1440

1446 Elizabeth
1478 Agnes Tanke
1521
1535 Margaret Sackville

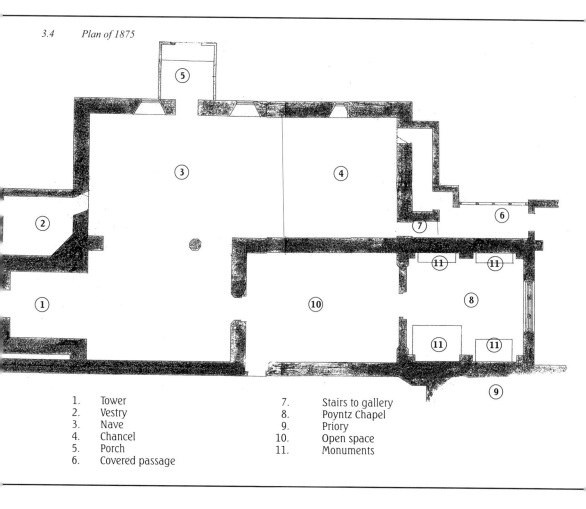

3.4   *Plan of 1875*

1.   Tower
2.   Vestry
3.   Nave
4.   Chancel
5.   Porch
6.   Covered passage
7.   Stairs to gallery
8.   Poyntz Chapel
9.   Priory
10. Open space
11. Monuments

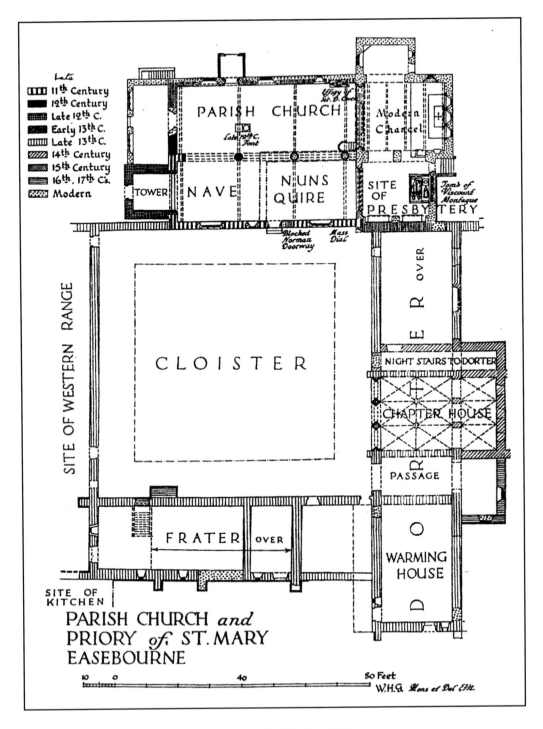

Late
- ⬛ 11th Century
- ⬛ 12th Century
- ⬛ Late 12th C.
- ⬛ Early 13th C.
- ⬛ Late 13th C.
- ⬛ 14th Century
- ⬛ 15th Century
- ⬛ 16th, 17th Cs.
- ⬛ Modern

PARISH CHURCH

Modern Chancel

Effigy of Sir D. Owen

Late 12th C. Font

TOWER — NAVE — NUNS QUIRE — SITE OF PRESBYTERY

Tomb of Viscount Montague

Blocked Norman Doorway — Mass Dial

SITE OF WESTERN RANGE

CLOISTER

DORTER OVER

NIGHT STAIRS TO DORTER

CHAPTER HOUSE

PASSAGE

FRATER OVER

WARMING HOUSE

DORTER

SITE OF KITCHEN

PARISH CHURCH and
PRIORY of ST. MARY
EASEBOURNE

10   0   40   80 Feet

W.H.G. Mens et Del Eft.

3.5   Evolution of the Church and Priory.

4. Roads and Footpaths

Origins of Turnpike

Sussex roads used to be notorious. A barrister wrote to his wife in 1690 that "the Sussex ways are bad and ruinous beyond imagination, I vow 'tis melancholy consideration that mankind will inhabit such a heap of dirt for a poor livelihood." Another writer of the same period said that in travelling through a slough of extraordinary miryness, it used to be called "the Sussex bit of the road."

From the medieval period onwards, parishes were ordered to maintain the roads within their boundaries, using compulsory unpaid labour under the direction of "waywardens". However this practice was so inefficient that from 1663, the main routes began to be turned into turnpikes. These were better roads maintained by paid labour funded by the tolls charged to travellers. The Highways Act of 1835 then placed the cost of repairing the minor roads on the parish rates.

One source of dispute between Easebourne and Midhurst had been the maintenance of the bridge over the Rother. This was resolved by arbitration around 1577 with each parish paying half. Since Midhurst was more likely to profit from through traffic, it had the best of the bargain.

Thomas Gardner's plan of 1719 showed that the London-Chichester road used to run locally via Chiddingfold and Lickfold, then over Bexley Hill and through Easebourne to Midhurst. However when in 1749 a Turnpike Trust was set up under a board of trustees, it was for "repairing the road from Hindhead Heath through Farnhurst (Fernhurst) Lane and Midhurst to the City of Chichester" because "many parts thereof so ruinous and deep in the winter season that carriages cannot pass without great danger and difficulty." At Hindhead, this connected to the London-Portsmouth road, (now the A3) which was also a turnpike.

In 1780 the northern end of the road was diverted to Milford and it was extended south to Delkey (Dell Quay). Two further Acts were passed in 1797 and 1818, but with the growth of the rail network in the 1860s, the roads became less important and when the powers of the Milford, Dell Quay Trustees lapsed on 1st November 1867 they were not renewed.

Route of the Road

The turnpike came through North Street Midhurst and crossed the Rother, the existing bridge being built in 1776. It went through Easebourne Lane, (also known as Mill Lane or North Mill Road), until it came to the corner of Wheelbarrow Castle where it turned left (the 25 inches to the mile Ordnance Survey map of 1874 shows a guidepost at this corner).

This particular road used to be known as Snow Hill, (also the name of a house on the corner). Wheelbarrow Castle is shown on the 1874 map but it relates only to a group of houses on a high bank on the north side.

The Tithe Map of 1847 shows a tollhouse on the south side of the road, by the junction with Dodsley Lane, near where the bus shelter now stands. It was built on a plot of land, with an area of 18 perches, (545 square yards) and was occupied by Thomas Dorey, the toll keeper. There was a small pound nearby for straying animals.

The tollhouse had a projecting centre bay where the money was collected, gates closing all the roads, and another guidepost pointing up the hill. A similar building still exists on the A272 Petersfield Road, about a mile west of Midhurst on the north side.

The turnpike then went up past the Union Workhouse and North Heath to the top of Henley Hill, a section originally known as Turnpike Lane. Then it plunged down steeply through Henley before continuing to Fernhurst. About 1790 plans were drawn up for a road running west of Turnpike Lane, crossing the Hospital drive (then a track leading to Redford) up across Madam's Farm, then over the brow of the hill down to Verdley Edge and north to the King's Arms and Fernhurst. Instead the existing curving road was built from the top of Henley Hill in 1825.

4.1   Approaching the village from the east, the gates needed to retain the deer in Cowdray Park were encountered. The view of the historic buildings was ruined by badly placed trees, just as the vista of the South Downs from this area is to be lost by new plantings.

4.2   A view of the other side of the gates reveals that a "Bye-Pass Bridge" was provided, following the advent of the thoughtless motorist. The ironwork of this historic device has recently been destroyed, but the superstructure remains.

4.3   Turning round, we can examine the two road junctions at the centre of the village, the Manor House being on the left. Resurfacing in 1976 raised the road level greatly here and created a dam for flood water from Easebourne Street (right). A modern road planing machine could restore the natural levels and thus the water flow.

4.4   This is the junction of the A272 and A286, so numbered in 1919. The numbers have been added on top of the arms; the post was moved close to North Mill, when footpaths were provided in the 1930s.

Stage Coaches

There was one daily stagecoach service from Chichester to London, passing one day through Midhurst and the next through Petworth. But the steep inclines of Budgenor Hill and through Henley must have presented serious problems.

In the second chapter of "A Tale of Two Cities", Charles Dickens describes the Dover Mail ascending Shooters Hill. It was so steep that the horses kept stopping and the three male passengers had to walk. Sometimes extra "cock horses" were attached to the team on the steepest sections, as in the rhyme "Ride a cock horse to Banbury Cross."

When descending a steep hill, skids were put under the wheels. These were long pieces of channel iron into which the wheels fitted and were held on by a chain, then the vehicle could slide down the hill.

Turnpike Regulations

There were set tolls for the various types of road users. The 1818 Act specified "For every horse or other beast drawing a coach, chariot, landau, chaise, hearse, curricle, gig or other carriage, the sum of nine pence. For every horse or mule, laden or unladen and not drawing, the sum of two pence; or for every ass laden or unladen and not drawing the sum of one penny."

Other animals were included, "for every score of oxen, cows, calves or other neat cattle, the sum of one shilling and eight pence; and so in proportion for the greater or lesser number (1d each).... For every score of sheep, lambs, hogs or swine, the sum of ten pence; and so in proportion for a greater or lesser number,' (½d each).

No windmill could be built within 200 yards of the road. Also 'any damage caused by animals or if they trespass, or if anyone leaves a wagon unharnessed except with accident or unloading or if they light a bonfire, or set off a squib, rocket or firework or play at football they will be subject to a fine not exceeding 40/- for the first offence or £5 for subsequent ones."

Other Roads.

In 1854 Mr. McClean surveyed the roads and footpaths of Easebourne. He listed 36 different routes, excluding the turnpike and the road through Cowdray Park. The total length was 20 miles, 99 yards.

Although many names have changed, Dodsley Lane is listed (the 1874 Ordnance Survey referred to it as Dawsley Lane). Despite not being a main route, it was expensive to maintain, between 1863 and 1866, repairs cost £37/9/4. Then in the late Victorian period houses were built along it.

The Cowdray Estate maintained the road through the Park. Under the 1835 Highway Act they became liable for a statute duty and in 1840, Alexander Brown the agent, requested that the Parish contribute £5 towards the costs. They agreed to this, since it was classified as a parish road for which they were responsible, and they continued to make payments at intervals.

Until after World War II there were deer in the park and the road was normally gated and closed at night. Two sisters lived in a cottage opposite the Chestnut Avenue and opened up for horse drawn vehicles, although they expected a penny tip. As traffic increased a bypass bridge was built with a cattle grid so that motor vehicles could be driven across. There were also gates near Benbow Pond and the Moor Farm road, and the three sets of gatekeepers had rather appropriate names, Steer, Deer and Buck!

During the World War II the gates were removed, reputedly by impatient Canadian tank drivers, and the deer were penned up in a small enclosure. Afterwards for a short period the gates were restored and the deer were allowed to roam freely again, but eventually they were culled and the road was opened up.

A more contentious issue was the road over Bexley Hill into Lickfold. In 1852 there was a debate as to how much of this route the parish was responsible for. Thomas Sanders thought they should only go as far as the Vining Stone Pit (just south of where a side road branches off to link with the A286). However Mr. Brown claimed the parish had always been responsible as far as the boundary stone near the bottom of Bexley Hill. "After a general discussion of this matter, the surveyors… determined that they repair the said road leaving to any party who might feel that they had any cause of complaint to take whatever cause they may consider proper."

Mr. Sanders also objected to Mr. McClean's 1854 survey of the footpaths. He claimed that three of these crossed his land, and the committee agreed that these were not parish paths. However they took the precaution to retain a local solicitor, Mr. Albery in case any proceedings were taken.

A different problem occurred in 1862 with the road leading from Woolavington Parish, (now West Lavington) past Great Todham Farm towards Heyshott. It was "reported to be seriously cut up and injured by the traffic of the contractors of the Mid Sussex and Midhurst Junction Railway" and the assistant waywarden took steps to compel the repairs to be done.

More Footpaths

In 1900 the Parish Council surveyed the footpaths again and published some details in the local press. The Cowdray Estate solicitor then wrote to them, asking that his letter be copied into the parish minutes.

He pointed out that many if not all of these footpaths passed over or through Lord Egmont's property and the Estate did not consider them to be public footpaths. They were kept open for the benefit of Estate tenants and workmen but he did not threaten legal action over the matter.

Despite this, fifteen years later the parish organised another survey and published it in five instalments; presumably Lord Cowdray was less concerned about trespass than his predecessor. The committee identified 33 footpaths, carefully describing each route and its condition. They "were greatly impressed by the beauty of many of the paths, and feel sure that their proper maintenance will add greatly to the popularity of the neighbourhood." They did think however "that stiles formed of creosoted rails… are a public nuisance and should not be permitted. Stiles should also be erected so that it is not necessary to be a practised athlete to get over or under them."

It is interesting to know how they would have coped with the aftermath of the Great Storm. A Parish Council report in February 1988 stated that two thirds of their 34 footpaths were still blocked. Also in a complaint which would be familiar to their predecessors, they claimed that the roads had deteriorated due to an increase in traffic although the budget was cut back or at best was at a standstill. However they thought that the roads in this part of Sussex were in a better state of repair than anywhere else.

Sources

Austen, Brian (2005) **Turnpike roads to Chichester. Midhurst and Petworth**. Sussex Industrial History, No. 35 28-40

WSRO Cowdray MSS 239,222.

Easebourne Tithe Map, 1847.

Ordnance Survey 25 inches to the mile map, 1874 (Sussex XXI.12)

Newman, Brenda (2004) **Fernhurst in Living Memory**, part 1. Highways old and new. The Fernhurst Society.

Dickens, Charles (1859) **A Tale of Two Cities**, Chapter 2.

Leslie, Kim (2003). **Bones that laughed and died**. Archives Magazine, November.

An Act of 18th May 1818 "for continuing and amending an Act of His present majesty for repairing the road from the north end of Farnhurst Lane, to the City of Chichester and from Chichester aforesaid to Delkey in the County of Sussex. To continue earlier Act and increase tolls to pay for it."

Minutes of the Easebourne Parish Council. 1822-1879.

5. Budgenor Lodge

Old Poor Law

For almost 200 years, Budgenor Lodge, originally known as 'The Easebourne House of Industry', was a refuge for needy people, first as a workhouse, then as an old people's home and finally as a hostel for the homeless. Following this it accommodated a Bible College before being transformed into a residential complex.

The building is particularly interesting, since it is one of the few surviving Georgian workhouses. It was built in 1793-4 under the Old Poor Law, the ancestor of our modern welfare system. This required that parishes looked after their own poor people and each year the Justices of the Peace ordered the churchwardens to appoint unpaid overseers who listed those needing help, raised a poor rate from the local property owners and distributed it.

Some money was given as 'outdoor' relief to help those living in their own homes while 'indoor relief' was used to accommodate paupers or vagrants in 'workhouses'. Here they were expected to work to defray the costs of feeding and housing them.

It was expensive having a workhouse for a few paupers, so groups of parishes began to pool their resources to run a central facility. The Chichester parishes did this in 1753 although they needed a private Act of Parliament to authorise this action.

Gilbert's Act of 1782 streamlined the process by allowing parishes to unite without requiring further legislation. Between 1789 and 1792, six such unions were set up in West Sussex of which Easebourne was the last and biggest.

Easebourne Union

On July 5th 1792, 16 local parishes (excluding Midhurst) signed an agreement to share costs and on August 1st, the Eighth Viscount Montague granted them a 99-year lease on land at a peppercorn rent. The building contract was signed on 7th February 1793 with Mr John Tidey, a "bricklayer" of Washington, Sussex, with a specification that ran to nearly 7000 words. Some of the original architectural drawings are preserved in a book by the Rev Arthur Young published in 1808,

Although most materials, stone, bricks, tiles, oak, lime and sand came from within two miles of the site, building was difficult. The weather was very wet and cold by turns, the French war had just begun and there were two local tragedies. Cowdray House, Lord Montague's seat burnt down in September 1793 and he drowned a month later. However Easebourne House of Industry opened on October 10th 1794, at a cost of £4005, £1205 above budget, with an extra £2156 for furnishings and raw materials for the paupers to work on.

Viewed from the road, the main building changed little, apart from a new front entrance, and a one storey high extension to the north of this until the recent development. The internal arrangement however was very different, incorporating a boardroom, dining rooms for the paupers, a bake house, a brew house and a laundry. Dormitories for the inmates were on the two floors above, together with a single-roomed hospital and a lying-in room for childbirth.

The wings on either side of the courtyard were mostly one story high, housing stables and workrooms. Under the clock tower there were two prison cells, ('the black hole'), a room of the dead, a washhouse, and a store for wood ash used in the laundry.

Organisation and Inmates

A board of 16 "guardians" controlled the workhouse. Each man was an unpaid elected representative of his parish, and there was a separate chairman or 'visitor'. The board appointed a 'governor' to run the house with his wife as 'matron' and a handful of staff.

The building was intended to hold 180 inmates, mostly children of 14 or under, and old people over 60. Handicapped adults were also admitted, together with the mothers of young children and women needed for domestic duties. At Easter 1795 there were 159 inmates, including 116 children, but by 1827 this had fallen to 65 with only 24 children.

The diet was barely adequate, providing on average about 2125 kilocalories per day. The main staple was bread since the newfangled potatoes were unpopular. Pigs were raised, and some mutton and beef were bought in and even live bullocks. A little milk and butter was produced but cheese was bought at local fairs. Sacks of boiling peas were purchased and cabbages were grown in the garden.

Tea and coffee were still luxuries, so beer was drunk, up to two pints a day per inmate, children having a weaker form known as 'small beer'. In 1795 it cost two shillings and eleven pence to accommodate one pauper for a week.

Working for their keep

Most paupers worked, making rough cloth, mops, shoes, clothes and hemp sacks or as hired labourers. Even children of five, picked wool, though most of those between three and nine attended the workhouse school, taught by an elderly woman.

Each parish bought its own raw materials and sold the products through merchants such as William Cobden, father of the famous reformer Richard. The paupers received one sixth of the proceeds as 'encouragement money'. Guardians who missed one of the monthly board meetings paid a 'forfeit' of five shillings, which was divided among those paupers too elderly or infirm to work.

However the whole system proved inefficient, and in 1799 the house was let out to a contractor who was paid a weekly fee for each inmate while taking any profits arising from their labour. Spiritual needs were met by a chaplain funded by Elizabeth Poyntz who had inherited the Cowdray Estate from her brother Lord Montague.

By 1834 there were so few children that the school had closed. Twenty or thirty single able-bodied men stayed in the house during the winter, and there were some married couples in their own rooms. All work was now agricultural, in the garden or on a 50-acre farm leased by the Governor. However the workhouse was running at a loss, the Union had agreed to pay the contractor for a minimum of 70 paupers each week, but the numbers were often less.

Midhurst Union

In 1834 in the face of soaring costs nationally, the new Poor Law was passed. Now any adult requiring relief was forced to enter a workhouse, but conditions were made so harsh that few would stay there voluntarily.

Easebourne Union was dissolved on 12th May 1835, being replaced by an enlarged one established under the new legislation. Ten more parishes were added, including Midhurst, which gave its name to the new incorporation. It was still run by a board of guardians but they were now responsible to the Poor Law Commissioners, a highly centralised organisation. Even trivial decisions had to be ratified by them, and many of their rulings were harsh and inflexible.

The guardians met weekly, taking copious minutes. A rigorous accounting system was introduced, an official order of 1836 listed 33 different forms to be completed and each parish had to provide quarterly returns.

EASEBOURNE UNION – FORMED 1792

1. BEPTON
2. CHITHURST
3. COCKING
4. EASEBOURNE
5. FARNHURST (FERNHURST)
6. IPING
7. LINCHMERE
8. LODSWORTH
9. LURGASHALL
10. SELHAM
11. STEDHAM
12. TILLINGTON
13. TRAYFORD (TREYFORD)
14. TROTTON
15. WOOLBEDING
16. WOOLAVINGTON (split 1869)

MIDHURST UNION – PARISHES ADDED IN 1835

17. DIDLING
18. ELSTEAD
19. HARTING
20. LINCH
21. MIDHURST
22. NORTH AMBERSHAM (COUNTY OF SOUTHAMPTON)
23. NORTHCHAPEL (until 1869)
24. ROGATE
25. SOUTH AMBERSHAM (COUNTY OF SOUTHAMPTON)
26. TERWICK

PARISHES ADDED 1869

27. GRAFFHAM
28. HEYSHOTT

PARCELS FROM OUTSIDE PARISHES

29. BIGNOR
30. STEEP

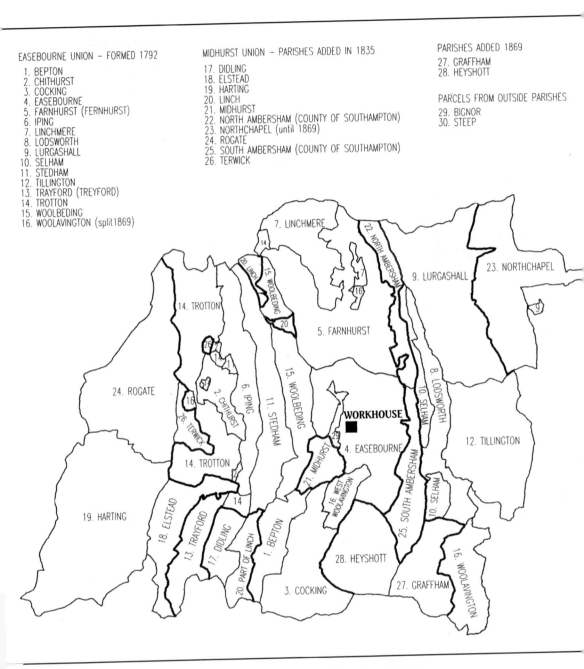

VIII.   *Parishes of the Midhurst and Easebourne Unions.*

5.1   *The east elevation is seen in about 1880 with the porters lodge on the left and the 1835 board room on the right.*
The children are playing cricket.

5.2   *A 2005 view from the same location reveals that the porters lodge demolition reveals the main entrance. The*
multitude of chimneys had been replaced by one from a central boiler. The building on the right had served as a chapel
and then a nursery school.

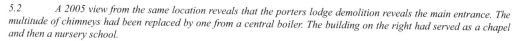

5.3   The clock carried the words "Time is short" and was mounted on the building which once housed the prison, mortuary and wash house for inmates. It is seen from the central court yard.

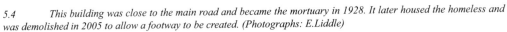

5.4   This building was close to the main road and became the mortuary in 1928. It later housed the homeless and was demolished in 2005 to allow a footway to be created. (Photographs: E.Liddle)

Harsh Conditions

The building was enlarged to take 350 inmates, the sexes were segregated with a wall built across the courtyard and children were separated from adults. These arrangements lasted many years. Inmates were virtual prisoners, wearing uniform and only being let out on special occasions while illegitimate children and their mothers had a particularly hard time.

The diet was strictly controlled and utterly monotonous. Bread, beer and other supplies were now brought from outside with contracts being renewed every six months. There were frequent disputes with the tradesmen about poor quality and delivery. One notorious butcher had the unfortunate name of 'A.Fish'!

Some inmates made shoes or clothes, but most had mundane jobs, picking 'junk' (old rope) to pieces, or grinding bones for fertiliser till this practice was banned in 1847. Many men worked on the land, in the garden or on local farms, while the women did domestic chores. Delinquents might suffer 24 hours in the prison cell on bread and water, or even be taken before the magistrate, but the situation eased in 1857 with the formation of the West Sussex Police Force.

Vagrants posed a real problem and threatened to swamp the workhouse in the late 1840s during the Irish potato famine. The situation was particularly acute in winter when there was little work available and eventually they were refused entry unless they had obtained prior authorisation.

To begin with boys and girls were taught separately but later there was a mixed class with a schoolmaster. 'Comprehensive' education was introduced in the 1850s whereby the boys spent most of their time outside learning agriculture while the girls were taught sewing and household skills. The workhouse school finally closed in 1896 with the children being sent to Easebourne Parish School.

Whenever possible older boys were apprenticed to firms such as the Great Grimsby Ice Company while some emigrated. Girls were sent to training homes before going into service, doing domestic work for the rich.

Staff

Very few staff were employed. There was a governor (called the Master after 1847) a matron, a porter, a schoolmaster, a schoolmistress and part time chaplain and medical officer. Morale was often low and there was a rapid staff turnover. One governor resigned over a pay dispute, and his successor was sacked for falsifying a beer invoice. Another was sued by a porter, who had been dismissed after being accused of misdemeanours such as peering through a crack in a door at the matron! Another porter died after 'running into a door', a third was sacked in a dispute over two pence while a fourth lost his job after making indecent advances to a woman visitor!

The guardians also supervised outdoor relief, administered by 'relieving officers'. These latter officials also authorised medical attention for the paupers, arranged their admittance to the workhouse and registered births, deaths and vaccinations. In later years they also enforced proper sanitation in the district and monitored school attendance.

Most relieving officers worked well, though one was sacked for drunkenness and others for incompetence and dishonesty. But the medical officers were less conscientious, few doctors would take this work on, and those who did often proved very lax.

Health care in the workhouse was limited, the standard medicine being cod liver oil. Imbeciles (individuals with learning difficulties) stayed in the house but most lunatics, (a general term for mental illness), were sent to overcrowded asylums such as Graylingwell in Chichester. Other handicapped or ill inmates went to appropriate institutions such as the Royal Sea Bathing Infirmary at Margate!

Modernisation

Very little money was spent on the building in Victorian times. The inmates did internal decoration and very occasionally the outside was painted by whichever firm submitted the lowest tender. There were frequent problems with the roof and for a time a rubberised patch was fitted.

Water supplies were uncertain. A new well was dug in the 1870s but this proved inadequate and supplies were piped from another source a mile up the hill. However in the building itself there was hot and cold water available on tap. Drainage was difficult too; this may account for the strange decision in 1895 to replace water closets with earth closets. But in 1905 mains water and drainage was at last provided.

Fire was a constant fear, particularly when Westhampnett Workhouse near Chichester burnt down in 1899. Various fire escapes and extinguishers were installed and in 1904 the porter was given a bicycle so he could summon help quickly. In 1911 a telephone was installed with an extension to the fireman's house. Motorcars began to be used around 1915 for moving patients and by the relieving officers. One of these men was injured in a car accident in 1920.

Humane Treatment

Inmates had few treats apart from Christmas dinner. However in 1872 Lord Egmont gave them a special meal including 80 pounds of beef to celebrate the recovery of the Prince of Wales, (later Edward VII) from illness.

Public opinion was slowly changing. In the 1890s many official restrictions were eased and public-spirited neighbours began providing treats and outings, particularly for the children. Individuals and concert parties gave entertainments, including demonstrations by the local gymnastic society. A Ladies Visiting Committee was formed which campaigned vigorously for better conditions and jobs for the young people. They even provided uniforms so that the boys could join the Scouts.

Old people could now roam freely outside, and aged couples shared a room once more. In 1913 a wooden balcony was erected on the south wall as a day room for old women too unwell to venture downstairs.

World War I and After

The first war bought many changes. In November 1914 nearly 100 Gordon Highlanders were billeted on the house, staying till February. For the rest of the war and well into the peace there was the constant problem of rising prices and inadequate supplies, particularly with coal, since over 100 tons were needed annually for heating and cooking.

By the 1920s most inmates were elderly and male, since the children were boarded out, being sent to schools in Surrey. Their mothers only saw them for two fleeting visits a year. The house was also certified to house 15 mental defectives, handicapped individuals needing supervision.

Although the workhouse ran smoothly, the Poor Law Administration was collapsing, particularly in urban areas. Reform was urgent and in 1930 the Boards of Guardians were replaced by new Public Assistance Committees.

Budgenor Lodge was fortunate to survive, since most other workhouses were closing down. Extensive repairs, rebuilding and modernisation were carried out including a new mortuary in outbuildings near the road, mains electricity and central heating. So much work was needed that the female residents were moved temporarily to other institutions.

The inmates enjoyed outings by charabanc to the sea, and received many gifts and entertainments from groups as diverse as the Women's Institute, the Scouts and concert parties. Money was also collected in a sheet on the verge from motorists driving back from Goodwood races up the steep hill near Budgenor Lodge. The wireless (radio) was enjoyed as early as 1924 and in 1934 regular visits began to the local cinema. These were later replaced by film shows in the house provided by a unit from St Richard's Hospital.

World War II

When war began, control of the workhouse passed to an emergency committee. For a few months Budgenor was classified as an emergency hospital, and the inmates expected to be evicted in favour of wounded servicemen. Some able bodied men were evacuated briefly, but the plans were then shelved. In 1941 the female residents were removed, and Budgenor was almost exclusively male for nearly 30 years.

Precautions were taken against air raids. A blast wall was built across the entrance and the ceilings were shored up with wooden posts. The old well was fitted with a petrol pump as an emergency supply and a fire watching post was built on the roof. There was even a first aid post in the outbuildings, although this was hardly used.

Severe rationing left the residents short of meat but they made a magnificent job of cultivating the gardens and were soon supplying the neighbourhood with vegetables. They also sold firewood, and several men roamed the Cowdray Estate searching for fallen wood and dead trees. Budgenor even began making and selling sweets. Easebourne Women's Institute valiantly attempted to give the inmates an annual treat despite the shortages, but there were no concert parties until after the war.

A County Council Home

In 1948 the Poor Law was finally abolished, but Budgenor continued as an old men's home. By now there were about 135 residents, but staffing levels were very low. The stoker normally worked at least 27 hours overtime a week with tasks as diverse as winding clocks, washing foul linen and serving food! Most residents only had a bath and clean clothes every fortnight.

But despite money shortages the next few years saw some major structural work, stabilising outside walls, rebuilding the kitchen and installing a lift. There were also battles with an infestation of ants and Death Watch beetles.

The final vestiges of the workhouse regime disappeared in the 1960s since the inmates were becoming too old to do useful work. Pig keeping was abandoned in 1963 after 170 years, and all gardening around 1969. The threat of closure now hung over the building and the last old men were moved out early in 1972 to the new Rother House in Midhurst.

A Hostel for the Homeless

Some homeless families were admitted in the early 1950s. Two housing units were installed in the outbuildings next to the mortuary; they were for women and children only, but some husbands slipped in illegally overnight.

Many families fell into rent arrears and there were problems with children. One woman regularly left her four to fend for themselves when she went out in the evenings, while another with ten was so cramped that Midhurst Council threatened to prosecute the County Council for overcrowding! Eventually two caravans were provided as overflow accommodation.

The units became so dilapidated that they were closed in 1964 and no more homeless families were admitted till 1969. They were now accommodated in the main building to the discomfiture of the elderly residents.

After these left in 1972, 15 living units were built for the homeless, later rising to 30 and a laundrette was provided. Once more Budgenor children attended Easebourne School and there was even a play school for the younger ones.

In August 1990 with an even greater problem of homelessness there was a call for Government funding to increase the number of living units to 45. But many people considered that the building was no longer suitable for housing, and it was decided to build new hostels in Midhurst and

Chichester. Some of the grounds were used for low cost housing, known as Hazlewood Close. The building finally closed on November 21st 1993, 199 years and 46 days after its opening.

Christ for the Nations UK

Three days earlier, Kevin Swadling had viewed the building with the intention of converting it into a Bible College. However it was not until October 1994 that he was able to take out a two-year lease, and work only began on January 14th 1995.

The task was daunting. The building was boarded up, extremely damp and very overgrown. But within six weeks, with help from volunteers and church groups, at least 20 of the 80 rooms were made usable and tuition started that September. The next academic year, 12 students enrolled and over 300 people attended short courses. Most of the premises were redecorated and carpeted and over 70 beds provided for students and visitors in addition to staff accommodation.

The building was purchased on March 27th 1997 for £300,000 nearly 75 times the cost of construction in 1794. By 2002 it was almost at full capacity with 48 students and 11 lecturers, both full and part time, and Kevin Swadling obtained planning permission to build ten new residential units in the grounds. However the cost, together with essential maintenance work was £1.5 million and he was unable to raise the money. Instead he sold the property to Dorepark Ltd of Fordingbridge, and bought the Royal Norfolk Hotel in Bognor Regis to be run jointly as a hotel and Bible College.

Residential Development

The college moved out in July 2004. The new owners planned to convert the premises into 54 residential units, and this met with the approval of Chichester District Council, Easebourne Parish Council and English Heritage. The premises were then sold on to BL Developments Ltd, but there was controversy about the outbuildings where the mortuary had been. Following the widening of the A286 in 1937, they abutted directly onto the road. They are not shown on the Tithe Map of 1847, but are marked on the 25-inch Ordnance Survey of 1874, so presumably they were built between those dates. They were demolished in the autumn of 2005 to provide a new footpath.

Work proceeded over the winter to convert the main structure into 39 residential units, with three new cottages near the road and a block of 12 affordable homes in the grounds on the north side. The very extensive renovation included re-roofing the building, renewing the drains, and providing 91 parking spaces.

History of Budgenor Lodge

A fully detailed history is proposed and expressions of interest are invited from readers. Please notify Middleton Press of your address and you will be sent details when they become available.

Sources
Most of the records are held in the West Sussex Record Office, whose staff have been unfailingly helpful and Petworth House. Other useful information came from Kevin Swadling, and BL Developments Ltd, and I am also very grateful to Jane Hunt for allowing me to look through her collection of cuttings from the Midhurst and Petworth Observer. The map was produced by Steve Moore.

6. King Edward VII Hospital

Origins

The inspiration for building the King Edward VII Sanatorium (later renamed the King Edward VII Hospital), may have come from His Majesty himself. At his accession, his financial advisor, Sir Ernest Cassell, placed £200,000 at his disposal for charitable purposes, and he used this to found the institution.

In his history, Dr. Sandy Large noted that the King was always interested in hospitals, particularly those treating pulmonary tuberculosis. Around 1900 there were 250,000 sufferers in Britain of whom 40,000 died each year. The symptoms began slowly with chronic tiredness, weight loss and coughing, sometimes producing blood, progressing to fever, sweating, wasting away, disablement and death.

Before effective drugs and surgical techniques became available, the usual therapy was fresh air, exercise and good food. Many sanatoria, particularly in Germany, provided these, acting rather like a modern health club. The King explained that he wanted to set one up in England "for the lower middle classes. Rich people can avail themselves of private sanatoria; the really poor are provided for by municipalities and through public benevolence; but between these there is a stratum of educated yet indigent patients such as teachers, clergymen, clerks, governesses, young officers, etc, who cannot afford the costs of a private sanatorium, whilst they are too proud or too bashful to avail themselves of public charity. My sanatorium is principally meant to take care of them."

Design and Site

An advisory committee met on 21st December 1901 and appointed a leading architect, Mr. Percy Adams, of Adams, Holden and Pearson, to draw up plans. He was assisted by a younger colleague, Dr. Holden, who probably did most of the work. The latter's obituary read "it may be said that Holden was pre-eminently the designer of the firm and that the aesthetic quality of their work was mainly due to him."

Three months later they found a 150-acre site, on Lord's Common Easebourne, the property of Lord Egmont, with a magnificent view south over Midhurst towards the Downs. However it was nearly 18 months before the building contract was signed with Messrs Longley of Crawley, due partly to obstruction by the agent Mr. Aman. There were also problems with the water supply and eventually a pumping station had to be built on Henley Common, feeding a reservoir on the hill.

Building

The King laid the foundation stone on 3rd November 1903. He had driven in an open carriage from Haslemere Station and the ceremony was held under a marquee with a service led by Bishop Wilberforce of Chichester.

Legend has it that during his visit the King examined the plans of the building and noted the absence of lavatories. These were hastily incorporated in bays off the main corridor. Three weeks later he made a surprise visit, distinguishing himself by climbing more scaffolding than any of his entourage.

The estimated cost was £96,000 with £9,650 for a separate chapel, but both projects were completed under budget. The architectural drawings covered 640 square yards of paper, the mile of road connecting the hospital to the Midhurst, Haslemere route needed 6,680 tons of stone, and the building incorporated 4,500,000 bricks, 500,000 tiles, 5000 tons of sand and 1000 tons of cement.

The most interesting event was the arrival of the boilers. They were towed from the railway by traction engine and were so large that the boiler house had to be built round them. This was sited

(continues on page 64)

6.1 This drawing, the brickwork notes and photographs 6.4 to 6.10 on the following pages are from March 2006 and are by R.G.Martin, secretary of the Sussex Industrial Archaeology Society.

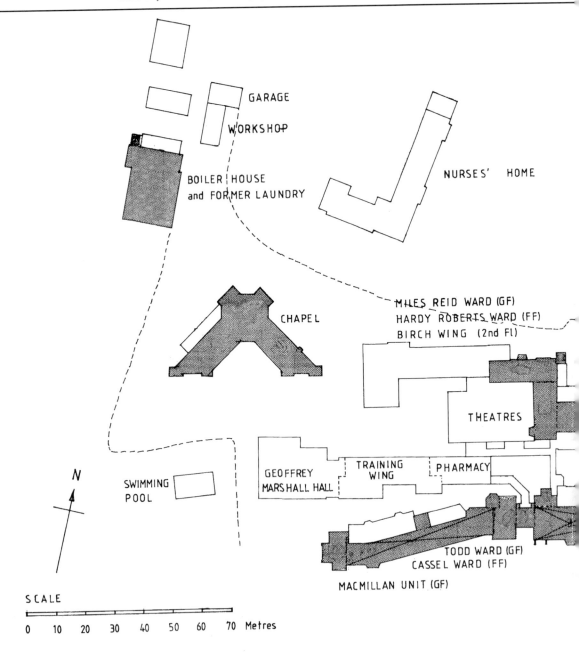

GARAGE

WORKSHOP

NURSES'   HOME

BOILER HOUSE
and FORMER LAUNDRY

MILES REID WARD (GF)
HARDY ROBERTS WARD (FF)
BIRCH WING (2nd Fl)

CHAPEL

THEATRES

TRAINING   PHARMACY
WING

GEOFFREY
MARSHALL HALL

SWIMMING
POOL

TODD WARD (GF)
CASSEL WARD (FF)

MACMILLAN UNIT (GF)

N

SCALE

0   10   20   30   40   50   60   70   Metres

BRICKWORK AT KING EDWARD VII HOSPITAL

The main building is H-shaped and three storeys high with a central corridor connecting the two wings. The south wing, which is 53 bays long (200m) is with all the wards facing south with balconies. The north wing contains the main entrance, administrative offices, dining hall, kitchen and staff quarters. An unusual building is the Chapel, which is L-shaped, with an octagonal chancel and two identical naves, at right angles to each other.

During the 18th and early 19th century, bricks in Sussex were traditionally burnt in up draught wood fired kilns. The method of stacking bricks in the kilns meant that the fly ash from the wood reacted at high temperature to produce grey headers. If brickwork is laid in English bond with alternate courses of headers and stretchers one gets an upleasant stripey effect. The popularity of Flemish bond where the headers are distributed in a pattern can be attributed to this phenomenon. It is also interesting to note that occasionally, particularly in Lewes, walls were built in header bond with a completely grey facade.

At the hospital, the architect had apparently seen the striped effect and liked the appearance of it. Although the external walls are (presumably) hollow and are built almost entirely in stretcher bond he has used two different types of bricks, one red and one grey, of unknown origin, and has perpetuated the stripey effect. The hospital is a large building and to break up the appearance of large areas of plain walls he has used several patterns of brickwork, with sometimes several different patterns on one elevation. These patterns are: 1. Alternate courses of red and grey bricks
2. One course of grey bricks with three courses of red bricks
4. Alternating red and grey bricks in each course
5. English bond with alternate red and grey courses
6. Flemish bond with grey headers and red stretchers.

The last two examples were not much used, presumably where solid walls were required. Subsequent extensions to the hospital, apart from the recent ones, have all perpetuated the brickwork patterns, not always with conspicuous success.

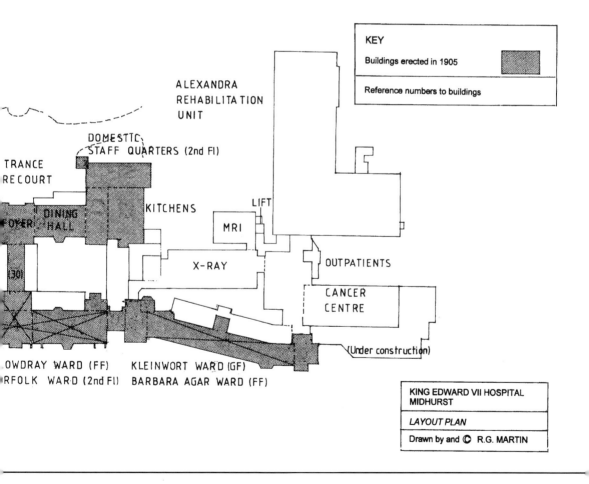

KEY

Buildings erected in 1905

Reference numbers to buildings

ALEXANDRA REHABILITATION UNIT

DOMESTIC STAFF QUARTERS (2nd Fl)

TRANCE RECOURT

DINING HALL

FOYER

KITCHENS

LIFT

MRI

X-RAY

OUTPATIENTS

CANCER CENTRE

(Under construction)

OWDRAY WARD (FF)   KLEINWORT WARD (GF)
RFOLK WARD (2nd Fl) BARBARA AGAR WARD (FF)

KING EDWARD VII HOSPITAL MIDHURST

LAYOUT PLAN

Drawn by and © R.G. MARTIN

6.2 Postcard view of the south elevation soon after completion.

*6.3   This card was posted in 1913 and features the Dining Hall and Kitchens:
Buildings 12, 14 and 18 on the plan.*

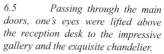

6.4 *The modest main entrance was on the north elevation of Building 11.*

6.5 *Passing through the main doors, one's eyes were lifted above the reception desk to the impressive gallery and the exquisite chandelier.*

6.6   The central entrance in South Wing, Building 1, with a despondent member of staff.

6.7   Even the ceiling of the staff dining hall in Building 12 had great style.

6.8　　　*Dormer windows and a Georgian influence was brought into Building 36, the Nurses Home.*

6.9　　　*Seen by few visitors was Building 20. This is the east side of the Laundry and Boiler House.*

6.10   The Alexandra Rehabilitation Centre had been built as the Midhurst Medical Research Institute. This is the east elevation of Building 43.

6.11   Seen from the south are the gender segregation wings provided for the chapel - Building 19.

6.12	*The chancel did not have the altar in line with either aisle; it is on the right, between two arches and below a sky blue dome. Dismantling was in progress.*

6.13	*Seven springs supplied water to the Hospital Pumping Station which was west of Henley Brick Yard and is shown on map II. It originally had a steam driven pump but this was replaced by electrical equipment in the 1950s, the double doors allowing movement of heavy items. The Hospital received mains water towards the end of the 20th century and the pump house was sold for residential purposes. It is seen in October 2006 and the control cabinets for the underground electric pumps are near the man on the left.*

(continued from page 55)

200 yards from the main building, being connected by a tunnel. As well as providing heat and hot water it generated all the electricity.

As completed, the main building looked much as it did 100 years later, with the administration block to the north connected by a corridor to the patients' area. This consisted of a three storey central block with two inwardly inclining wings two storeys high, built with alternating dark red and salmon pink bricks, a red tiled roof, white facings and green shutters.

Ian Nairn writing in Pevsner's guide describes it as "immense but not at all crushing, certainly one of the best buildings of its date in the country... a mixture of gabled free Tudor and artless classical motifs has been used on a fifty-three bay facade so that it always feels friendly and humane. The whole group is a model of how to build very large institutions."

Each resident had a single room facing south, with a partitioned balcony, sunblind, radiator, electric light and washable wallpaper, while the corridors and stairways were arranged so that each inmate could leave the building without passing a ward housing the opposite sex or different class. There was an electric lift in the central block and the main rooms were heated with coal fires.

A Portsmouth brewer, Sir John Brickwood, donated the chapel, described by Nairn as "a very carefully thought out building." It was in the shape of a V, with a nave for each sex and at the apex, a domed octagonal chancel and stone pulpit for outdoor services and the inner sides had open arches to provide maximum ventilation. The woodwork of the pulpit and altar were by C. R. Ashbee's Guild, and the chandelier in front of the altar was described as "big with very delicate ironwork, typical of 1900, Art Noveau in effect but not in style."

A disappointing feature of the workmanship was the number of problems that occurred within a few years of completion. In 1909 a leak in the chapel roof was repaired with concrete, then in 1910 dry rot was discovered in one staircase, and two years later in some of the ceilings and balconies. The repair bill came to £3,800.

The gardens were more successful. They were planned by Miss Gertrude Jekyll of Godalming, who had worked on 120 country houses with Sir Edwin Lutyens. A series of terraces, separated by stonewalls, were built on the south side, with lawns, flowerbeds, shrubs and aromatic herbs. However, north of the hospital the trees were very close to the building and were only thinned out in 1911.

Prewar World War I Days

The date of the official opening was decided at the last moment. The King and Queen arrived at Midhurst Station at 4 p.m. on 13th June 1906 and were met by the local dignitaries. They completed their journey by carriage escorted by a mounted troop of the Sussex Imperial Yeomanry. The ceremony took place in the dining hall with 250 guests and the King reaffirmed his wish that the Sanatorium should cater for professional people of slender means.

After the inauguration, Edward VII gave permission for the King's Sanatorium, as it was then known to take his name. The Advisory Committee was reorganised as the Executive Committee, then in 1913, when the Sanatorium received its Royal Charter of Incorporation from George V, it became the Council. It handled administration and finance and was advised on medical matters by the Consultants. There were also a number of influential and well disposed people who were listed as "Members of the Institution"

Dr. Noel Bardswell was appointed Medical Superintendent in 1905 at the age of 33 and stayed for 12 years. Although medically qualified, most of his work was administrative, and to begin with he had only one clinical assistant. He used to dress informally and once overheard the King say "Who is this burglarious looking tramp following us around?"

Another long serving member of staff was Mrs. Hatchell who became matron in 1908 at a salary of £80 per annum. Although she had no formal training, she supervised two sisters and eight nurses and a domestic staff numbering about 50.

The Midhurst Regime

Originally there were two classes of patients, "A" paying two guineas a week, and "B" paying eight, although the second category was later abolished. In the first year, 161 patients were treated, numbers rising from 30 on the opening day until by March 1907 all 100 beds were full. These came almost exclusively from the professional classes; others such as Count Albert Mensdorff's valet were excluded. Patients with more advanced tuberculosis were rarely accepted since this was not intended "to be a home for the dying", instead the emphasis was on treating the early stages of disease and individuals were only expected to stay for four months.

Dr. Bardswell insisted that each patient had a daily period of complete rest, when even talking and reading was forbidden. Their diet was carefully regulated to avoid putting on too much weight; they had daily baths or showers, and were encouraged to take exercise. This included gardening and walking along measured pathways, although cycling was prohibited. Alcohol was forbidden and the sexes were strictly segregated apart from chance meetings while strolling outside.

Before they were discharged, they were given advice on maintaining a healthy life style. Dr Bardswell tried to find them jobs and sent them an annual questionnaire on their progress. A research programme showed the success of the regime in less advanced cases, and in 1914 the British Medical Journal commented, "enough has been said to convince the most sceptical that the Midhurst Sanatorium has fully justified its existence."

Economic Pressures and World War I

There were already economic pressures. Much of the income came from the interest on £60,000, the balance of the endowment after paying for the building and equipment. However by 1912 there was a yearly deficit of £320 before taking depreciation into account.

Sir Ernest Cassell suggested that the income would be increased if additional patients were treated. However in 1913, he rejected a plan costing over £13,000 for 40 more beds and 17 extra staff. Mr. Isodore Salmon, an expert in hotel management, reduced costs by £500 by making two redundancies, redeploying staff and reducing the milk order, but then Sir Ernest gave a further endowment of £25,000.

However when war was declared on 4th August 1914, the Sanatorium faced a bleak future. At an emergency meeting two days later, the Council noted that several staff had already enlisted and they feared that the supply of patients would diminish or stop altogether. To make matters worse, their principal suppliers had repudiated their contracts, making it difficult to obtain or pay for food and other necessities.

They decided to close the Sanatorium temporarily and send the patients home, leaving the building in the care of Dr Bardswell and a small staff so that the others could join up. But on 8th August Lord Cowdray wrote, offering to underwrite the Sanatorium's expenses during the war if it stayed open. This proved to be very generous, since the annual deficit exceeded £2000.

In November 1914 the War Office offered to take over the building to treat sick and wounded soldiers. The King gave his approval, then a new plan was suggested, 50 members of the services with tuberculosis would be treated instead, although since they could no longer segregate the sexes, the other beds would only be used by male civilians. But following further discussions, in May 1915 the Sanatorium reverted to its original role of treating tuberculosis in professional people of limited means. Some officers were admitted, but there were no privates or non-commissioned officers.

New Developments

Early X ray machines were of limited value in studying the chest since they required an excessive exposure time, but by 1916 the consultants were requesting one of the new, improved instruments. This was finally installed in 1920 at a cost of over £500 although it was a year before a trained engineer was employed to take the films.

One of its uses was to monitor artificial pneumothorax, a therapy that had been introduced to Midhurst in 1918. Air was introduced into the chest cavity to collapse an affected lung and expedite healing. The process was repeated at intervals, since otherwise the lung would re-inflate, so this was regularly checked by X ray.

Dr R. R. Trail was appointed as superintendent at the age of 30 in 1924, at a salary of £1000 per annum. Staff morale was low following the resignation of his predecessor who had forfeited the confidence of the Council, but he soon restored a good working environment, tightening up the Midhurst regime and replacing unsatisfactory members of staff. He insisted on seeing the bed patients personally every day and the others at least once a week.

One innovation was chest surgery. In 1928, a leading thoracic surgeon, Mr. Tudor Edwards became a visiting consultant and he was to have a major influence. Irretrievably diseased lungs could be collapsed permanently, either by thoracoplasty, (the removal of ribs) or phrenic avulsion (the destruction of the nerve supply to part of the diaphragm to paralyse it.) Patients had been referred to the Brompton Hospital for these operations, but in February 1934, the Sanatorium opened its first operating theatre in a converted dental room.

Sir Geoffrey Todd

But before the surgical unit was ready, Dr Trail had resigned. He was succeeded by a 33-year old Australian, Dr (later Sir) Geoffrey Todd, who stayed as Medical Superintendent for 37 years. Unlike his predecessors he had no outside work and devoted himself to the Sanatorium. Apart from medical duties he was expected to keep a check on the pigs, poultry, garden and grounds, report on the weather, water supply, milk and food, the health, entertainment and welfare of the staff, the cooking arrangements, the accommodation, heating and lighting and the proceedings of the General Purposes Committee which was run by the patients.

There were three wards for men and three for women, and the sexes were still segregated. There were no effective drug therapies, so apart from surgery the Midhurst Regime of fresh air, rest, good food and graduated exercise continued although patients were no longer hosed down in the mornings "to harden them up!"

Staff kept apart from patients at meal times to reduce the risk of infection and the walls of the dining hall were regularly washed down with disinfectant. Domestics moved round the hospital using passages in the basement to avoid encountering patients in the corridors.

Entertainments included billiards, whist and bridge, listening to the wireless with headphones at the bedside, and from 1938 watching television. Concert parties visited every fortnight during the winter and film shows were given every week. Gentlemen kept to the left of the hall with ladies to the right while Dr. Todd sat at the rear with his mother and other medical staff, to keep watch on behaviour!

Alcohol was still prohibited, and intercepted bottles were held in "bond" until the patient's discharge. On leaving they were given instructions on convalescence, "never run when you can walk, never walk when you can stand, never stand when you can sit and never sit when you can lie."

Modernisation

Dr Todd also turned his attention to modernisation. With the new consultant radiologist, the oddly named Dr J V Sparks, he upgraded the X ray department to state of the art. In 1937 the Sanatorium electricity supply was connected to the grid, (the original turbines were retained for emergencies), and the building was rewired. The laundry and kitchen were completely remodelled, and a new policy of bulk buying raised the efficiency of the catering service fourfold.

Improvements in the operating theatre led to increased usage; there were 95 procedures in 1936-7 but 120 two years later. The nursing staff increased to 26 and with patients spending longer in the Sanatorium, the pressure on beds increased. The consultants argued for a new 25-bed wing but the Council refused, citing insufficient funds and doubting whether the infrastructure could support the increased numbers. After much discussion it was decided to build a new nurses' home, releasing extra space for patients. Work began in August 1939, and despite delays caused by the outbreak of war and the extreme winter of 1939-40, it opened a year later.

World War II

The Munich crisis of 1938 had forced the Council to prepare for war. An ARP (Air Raid Precautionary) unit was set up, the staff dug trenches in the woods and food was stockpiled. The Government had planned to use the Sanatorium as a chronic general hospital serving Southampton, a suggestion the Council thought was a gross misuse of their resources.

The outbreak of war brought more bizarre ideas; some naval officers tried to commandeer the site as a signal station, and there were plans to turn half the facilities into a maternity unit. Instead, it was then decided to use 60 beds for surgical chest cases with the remaining 60 reserved for tuberculosis. Accordingly during the early part of the war, the Sanatorium was half empty, although the Government paid for the unused surgical wards.

Meanwhile the ARP unit was reconstituted and a section of the Home Guard set up. The trenches were renovated, sand bags were provided; an air raid shelter was constructed in the basement for patients and blackout material purchased to cover the windows. However it was only in August 1940 when the Battle of Britain began and Tangmere airfield was bombed, that casualties began to arrive.

Attacks on Portsmouth and Southampton added to the load, and while only 100 operations were performed in the first 12 months of the war, this rose to over 500 in the last. There were 2,340 in all, of which 56% were on service personnel, the number of theatre nurses was doubled, a masseuse was employed to assist post-operative recovery and the artist Adrian Hill introduced art therapy, teaching patients how to sketch and paint.

Apart from casualties, many service and merchant navy personnel were admitted with tuberculosis. Forty-four thoracoplasties were performed in the first year of the war, rising to 116 in the last. There were also more cases of cancer and pneumonia and in 1944 the War Office paid for two Nissen Huts and staffing to treat 30 more patients.

Post War Recovery

Even before hostilities ceased, the Ministry of Pensions recommended erecting a new surgical wing to replace the temporary accommodation but it was January 1947 before agreement was reached with the Council. The facilities opened in July 1949, providing 32 rooms for patients undergoing major surgery, 28 rooms for staff accommodation and a pathology laboratory.

The advent of the National Health Service (NHS) threatened the independence of the Sanatorium. The Health Minister, Aneurin Bevan, was invited to visit the premises in June 1947, and was told of its special relationship with the monarchy and the policy of the treatment of patients of limited means, the impressive war record and the new surgical wing.

He agreed that although it would still be under the Ministry of Health, it could operate outside the NHS, free of control and supervision by the Regional Health Board. However they would pay for some NHS patients and the Ministry of Pensions would use up to 60 beds for service personnel.

The introduction of the anti-tuberculosis drug Streptomycin in the mid 1940s had an even more profound effect. Previously fatal forms of the disease could now be treated, and although some resistant bacilli emerged, they could be controlled by a combination of drugs.

A New Role

On August 1st 1956, the Queen visited the Sanatorium to celebrate its fiftieth anniversary. She had agreed to become its president, the fifth monarch in succession to grant that honour.

Among those greeting her was Geoffrey Todd, who had been knighted in 1951. He sat on every British committee dealing with tuberculosis and other chest diseases and had an international reputation. He had made Midhurst a centre of excellence, attracting large numbers of foreign doctors, particularly from Australia. In 1962 he hosted a three-day international conference on the treatment of tuberculosis followed two years later by another on asthma, and in 1966 a symposium on "Carcinoma of the bronchus and other malignant conditions of the lung."

The work of the Sanatorium was altering rapidly. In 1951 it had a waiting list of 100, with tuberculosis sufferers filling 168 of the 180 beds, but ten years later they were using less than 15. The introduction of newer drugs such as Isoniazid and PAS had a dramatic effect, long bed rest was unnecessary and patients were discharged more quickly. Surgery was also facilitated, for since infection could be totally eradicated from damaged lung tissue, this could be removed without risk of spreading the disease, or even left where it was.

In 1964, the Queen granted a supplemental charter changing the Sanatorium's name to "King Edward VII Hospital". This recognised its altered role in treating other thoracic disease or patients with quite different conditions.

Support Services and Nurses

With this wider range of work it was necessary to increase support facilities. Dr Ian Gordon, another Australian clinician who came to Midhurst in 1949, took charge first of the radiography department, then the pathology laboratory, which he ran until 1991. X Ray examinations expanded to include the gut, urinary tract, gall bladder, bones and muscles. Laboratory services included bacteriology, assessment of anti-tuberculosis drugs, histology (microscopic examination of body tissue) and haematology (clinical investigation of blood). There was also a respiratory physiology laboratory studying how well patients could breathe.

It was difficult to attract nurses to this rural area despite the good living conditions. One inducement was to offer specialised training for the Certificate of the British Tuberculosis Association, (later the Thoracic Nursing Certificate), and the King Edward VII Sanatorium Certificate (given to those completing 18 months of postgraduate training). A pupil-nurse programme was also set up in 1964 leading to the State Enrolled Nurse Certificate. There were only ten candidates in the first year, but numbers soon grew to 20 or 30 with many entrants coming from Malaysia and Nepal. The school closed in 1989 although University of Surrey students continued to do practical training in the hospital.

RAF Wing

A link was established with the RAF in the 1930s, and many service personnel were nursed during the Second World War. Then in 1964 a RAF chest unit was opened under the direction of Group Captain Ian Cran, (later Air Commodore Cran).

Air Force personnel with chest problems were flown in from all over the world; some emergency cases even landing by helicopter on the cricket field. Ian Cran died suddenly in 1978 and was succeeded by Squadron Leader, (later Wing Commander) Andrew Hopkirk, who ran the unit until it closed in March 1994.

New Building

There was considerable building during this period, although care was taken to see that the new work toned in with the old. The nurses' home was extended, two new wards were built on the north side, together with the Geoffrey Marshall Recreation Hall paid for by Sir Halford Reddish, Chairman of Rugby Portland Cement. There was also a lecture hall, bungalows for the staff, an open-air swimming pool, a new lift in the main building and oil fired boilers to replace the original coal ones.

In March 1957, as a result of fund raising by Bishop Bell of Chichester, the open sides of the chapel were glassed in, making it possible to hold services indoors. The east nave was used by the Anglicans, the other was given to the Roman Catholics, making this one of the few bi-denominational churches in England.

Fresh Challenges

But it was increasingly difficult to maintain full occupancy of the hospital; for while there were many more patients, they stayed for a much shorter time than their predecessors. The RAF was financing its ward, but the army had its own facilities and did not refer patients to Midhurst, while the Pension Board only paid for 85 beds instead of 120. Even private patient numbers had fallen to an average of 20.

In response to this situation, the Association of Friends of the Hospital was founded in 1966 to raise funds for equipment and amenities for patients and staff. It began with a donation of £20,000, and was launched with a cricket match and a fete.

A report to Council in 1968 recommended that the Hospital should be able to handle all kinds of medical and surgical cases, without abandoning its primary interest in chest disease. It suggested giving part time appointments to consultants working locally and in London in order to increase the number of referrals.

One of these new contacts was Professor John Charnley, a pioneer in hip joint replacement surgery. He decided to extend his work to Midhurst, operating for the first time in December 1969. He performed over 1300 procedures in the King Edward VII Hospital with only two fatalities, a testimony to his skill and the level of care.

Great improvements were also being made to the X ray department and operating theatres, due partly to a £50,000 donation from Marks and Spencer. But the greatest benefactor was Sir Halford Reddish who gave funds for new operating theatres and a central sterile supply department. In 1977 he provided a whole body scanner, and when he died in 1978, he left money for a new outpatients department, four consultation suites and an oncology (cancer) unit with a linear accelerator for radiotherapy. The Prince of Wales opened this facility on July 31st 1980, naming it the Mountbatten Wing.

Midhurst Medical Research Institute

In 1969 Sir Halford also gave £5 million to found a medical research institute for the study of cardio-respiratory disease; this was to operate independently of the hospital but maintain close links with it. The idea provoked some scepticism but was strongly supported by the Duke of Norfolk, chairman of the Council. Sir Geoffrey Todd became the first administrator after retiring as Medical Superintendent of the Hospital in December 1970, and Dr Gordon Cumming of Birmingham University was appointed Director in November 1971.

Building began the next April on a site northeast of the main building, and staff began moving in at the end of the year. They took over the building in April 1973 and the Queen opened it on 2nd November. Extra precautions were taken during her visit, due to local protests against animal experimentation.

Initially there were 60 staff and five senior clinical investigators who were also responsible for patients on one ward. In addition to pure research, the Institute provided cardiac, pulmonary and radioisotope clinical investigations, and the pathology department was housed in its basement.

Research interests ranged from studies of the biochemistry of the heart and new methods for diagnosing tuberculosis, to making respiratory measurements in volunteers. Groups, such as smokers and firemen, were examined at six-month intervals to see what changes were occurring in their lungs. School children were examined to assess the incidence of smoking, and estimates were made of the tar and carbon monoxide exposure in subjects presented with a variety of cigarettes.

Detailed measurements were also obtained from casts of the airways, made by injecting plastic into lungs then dissolving away the tissue. Computer analysis of these data, including a method originally developed to study river systems, led to a new theory of how gases mix within the lung.

One million pounds of Sir Halford's endowment had been used to build and equip the Institute, and the remainder was invested to provide an income. However this was a period of rapid inflation, the pound falling in value by almost three quarters between 1970 and 1980 and the financial future became insecure. There were even economies with the air conditioning system, designed in an era of cheap fuel before the oil crisis of 1973.

The management were faced with a harsh choice of making staff redundant and reducing the level of research, or joining with another organisation. Following negotiations with the Cardio-Thoracic Institute of the University of London, a merger was completed on 30th November 1984, and the Midhurst Institute's assets were transferred. It closed on 30th September 1987 with the retirement of Dr. (now Professor) Gordon Cumming, although he then formed a new unit in the Robens Institute, at the University of Surrey, which continued research into smoking until 1990. The building meanwhile had been converted into the Alexandra Rehabilitation Centre, opened by Princess Alexandra in 1989.

Douglas Macmillan Unit

In 1986 the Research Institute and Hospital collaborated to establish a Douglas Macmillan Continuing Care Unit. This catered for terminally ill cancer patients, providing pain relief, improving the quality of life, and giving support for families. Patients were visited in their homes and when the burden of care became too great, they were admitted to a hospice ward with five beds. This was believed to be the only such unit operating within a general hospital.

Within ten years the service expanded, with more beds, two consultants, four home care sisters, a principal social worker and a voluntary services organiser, while spiritual support and counsel was given by the chaplain, the Vicar of Easebourne. Fundraising included a charity shop in Midhurst and special events such as a Christmas tree, "The Tree of Hope", erected outside Easebourne Priory.

New Facilities

In 1982 a day care ward was opened to accommodate patients undergoing minor surgery. There were also new diagnostic facilities such as fibre optic endoscopy, (a flexible probe which visualises the interior of the body), a new whole body scanner, a mammography unit for breast screening, a MRI (magnetic resonance imaging) scanner and new cardiac X ray equipment.

But there were unavoidable costs. Until the 1980s the hospital had enjoyed Crown Immunity, which exempted it from many regulations affecting other institutions. Now it had to comply with all the rules on health, safety, and employment law, and was increasingly subject to European legislation.

The Great Storm of 1987

There was also a natural disaster, the great storm of the 15th and 16th of October 1987, the worst to strike Southern Britain since 1703.

The Hospital suffered considerable structural damage and thousands of trees were uprooted, blocking every road, but access was soon re-established due to the heroic efforts of the works and gardening staff. Telephone lines were restored next day, but it was over a week before mains electricity was reconnected. Many of the nurses remained on duty to cover for those who could not get in, while others had to walk considerable distances scrambling over tree trunks and debris.

Financial Restructuring

The Hospital still attracted many patients, but income was steadily falling In 1975 the average length of stay was 23.7 days, but this dropped to 14.1 in 1980 and 8.8 by 1988. and many beds were unoccupied.

There were fewer NHS referrals as local health authorities also came under financial strain. Attempts were made to attract more private patients; facilities were upgraded and private bathrooms were provided wherever possible. In 1982 a Hospital Strategic Plan was implemented with the aim of increasing bed occupancy from 120 to 140, largely by improving links with local consultants. The post of Chief Executive was created, and Mr. John Goldsworthy, was appointed in 1983.

For a time there was an improvement, out patient attendances rose 29.5%, between 1981 and 1985 and admissions increased by 25.6%, of whom nearly half were private patients. About 100 hip replacements were performed in NHS patients from Brighton, Worthing, Portsmouth and even Bath.

But by the end of the decade there were more problems. Despite a turnover of £8.1 million in 1989-90 there was a deficit of £800,000. This was more than covered by charitable giving and bequests, but it set a worrying precedent. Things improved the next year, with a shortfall of only £244,000 while £865,000 was raised. The Hospital also attracted Royal patronage; the Queen visited on July 12th and on the 14th Prince Charles attended a fund raising polo match in Cowdray Park.

However when a new chief executive, Paul Benson, was appointed in April 1992, there were serious problems. The recession had affected private health care, and the Sherburne, a new private hospital in Chichester, was competing for business. The deficit had risen to £900,000 and although this was covered by fund raising and bequests, urgent action was deemed necessary. Sixty staff posts were lost, including some by compulsory redundancy, and two wards were closed.

The next year's deficit soared to £1.7 million, though this included redundancy payments, and it was not all covered by voluntary giving, leaving a shortfall of almost £1 million. By contrast 1993/4 saw an operating surplus of £3000, while the financial appeals were being handled more professionally with the establishment of a Development Office and the King Edward VII Development Trust. That year £1 million was raised with charitable events including a concert and firework display at the Cowdray Ruins and a ball at Goodwood House. Even better results were obtained in 1996/7 with a total of £2.5 million, while £1.24 million was donated the year after.

In December 1994 a three-year business plan was adopted. This committed the hospital to develop cardiac and thoracic services, while maintaining links with the NHS. A contract was won to provide cardiac services for the Isle of Wight, while 4,500 outpatients and 1,400 inpatients from West Sussex attended the Hospital. There was still a deficit of £500,000, but in the next year a profit of £28,000 was made.

Lavinia, Duchess of Norfolk

Lavinia, Duchess of Norfolk died in December 1995. She had been vice president of the Hospital for 20 years following the death of her husband, the 16th Duke, and for most of this time she was chairman of the Council, renowned for her fresh approach to business.

Her interest went back 58 years to when she married Bernard, a member of the Council. The Norfolk family had been associated with the Hospital since 1913 when the Royal Charter was granted, and King George V had chosen the 15th Duke as one of the first Members of the Institute. She herself had become a Member in 1950 when she was also appointed Lady Visitor.

Lord Egremont became vice president in her place His ancestral home, Petworth House, was only a few miles from the Hospital and he had always taken a keen interest in its affairs.

Project Heartbeat

Project Heartbeat began in 1995. Originally it was just intended to upgrade the cardiac facilities of the Hospital, diagnostic, therapeutic and surgical. These latter suffered a setback on 7th January 1996 when fire broke out in the operating complex. The surgeons' rest room was totally destroyed and heat and smoke damage seriously affected the surrounding area, putting all four operating theatres out of commission. However two were back in limited use within three days, and by the middle of February the unit was completely reinstated.

The project evolved into a £2.5 million programme involving enhancement and refurbishment of the building. The outpatient department was improved, a lift and staircase were installed at the east end of the hospital, and an additional corridor and new coronary care unit with direct ambulance access were provided. The cardiac ward, Barbara Agar, was remodelled to provide twelve single rooms with en-suite facilities, a six-bedded ward and a three-bedded high dependency unit.

Following the completion of this work, the patient workload increased by 4.7% with 26.5% more day patients, 242 cardiac operations, (up by a quarter compared with the previous year), and 1300 orthopaedic procedures.

In a final phase in 2002, another £1.3 million was spent on two "Thunderbird Two Modular Cardiac Catheters" for diagnostic work. This boosted confidence at a time when St Richard's had announced an extension of its cardiac services, a programme which threatened to take patients away from Midhurst.

Sherburne Hospital

On 20th March 1996 the Hospital purchased Chichester Independent Hospitals Ltd, which owned the 49-bed Sherburne Hospital. In its three years of existence, it had had a noticeable effect on private patient admissions at Midhurst, but now the intention was that the two hospitals should work to their strengths without competing. In addition, since the King Edward VII Hospital was a registered charity, any income derived from the Sherburne could be covenanted and not taxed.

Initially the acquisition was a success. In 1997/8 and 1998/9 the Sherburne produced surpluses of £800,000 and £965,000, and there were advantages in being able to share equipment and staff. However in November 2000 it was sold to the Nuffield Group. It was no longer seen as a threat to Midhurst, and the money raised from the sale was used to upgrade facilities and cover debt.

Financial Crisis

There had been another financial crisis in 1998/9 with an operational deficit of £1.7 million. This was due to a further reduction in bed occupancy and a £2.5 million shortfall in Project Heartbeat. Lin Merritt, (the former manager of the Sherburne), who became chief executive in 1999, warned of the serious consequences on the local economy should the Hospital close. With 425 full and part time staff, and a £8 million wage bill it was one of the largest employers.

In July 1999, West Sussex Health Authority predicted a £10 million shortfall in its own finances over the next four years. The Health Minister, Frank Dobson did not like the use of non-NHS providers, so it intended to make less use of Midhurst in future. This was despite the latter's investment in new equipment and its record on cardiac investigation and surgery which was well above the national average. As a result the Hospital decided to cut the number of its beds from 115 to 92.

The Health Authority also proposed that from April 2000, the King Edward VII Hospital would cease to treat emergencies. It was dealing with 600 such admissions each year and 100 non-emergency cases from an area stretching between Storrington and Rogate, and from Fernhurst to Cocking. However it did not meet the criterion of the Joint Consultants Committee that hospitals could only provide the full range of emergency facilities if they served a population of at least 200,000. However St. Richard's met this condition, and by diverting these extra cases there, its position would be strengthened and the Health Authority would save £500,000 annually, although ambulance journeys would be prolonged by an average of eight minutes.

Despite opposition from the local Community Health Council, GPs, clergy and MPs during a two-month consultation period, the emergency services were duly terminated. In consequence, Midhurst lost two consultant and three senior house officer posts although in compensation they were awarded NHS contracts worth £2 million, similar in value to what they had forfeited.

Hurst Park

Faced with the need to raise £10 million for new equipment and services, the Hospital trustees approached a firm of chartered surveyors to advise on the best use of the site. As a result, in November 1999, they sought outline planning permission to replace 28 surplus staff houses with new prestige dwellings with their own access road, pond and village green. This was granted in May 2000, but the local parish council condemned the plan "as a stockbroker enclave more appropriate for Esher than Easebourne" and there were also complaints from the Sussex Downs Conservancy Board.

However by August 2001, Berkeley Homes South had completed a show house, saying how "rare it was to find a brown field site surrounded by such beauty." The completed estate consisted of 28 houses, cottages and bungalows in the form of a crescent round a pond, but six months after completion, eight properties were still unsold and they were being offered at a reduced price.

There were also problems with the water supply. Following the operating theatre fire of 1996, the Hospital had been connected to the mains and two new reservoirs provided. However in July 2003, a water main burst in Fernhurst, and the estate suffered supply problems for a week.

Brief Recovery

In 2000, the financial situation eased. To reduce their waiting lists, Portsmouth awarded a contract for 180 eye operations, and patients were also transferred from the Community (formerly Cottage) Hospital while this was refurbished. The next winter, with local hospitals facing a bed crisis, a ward was set aside to accommodate the extra cases.

By August 2001, the position had improved further. Lin Merritt (now Lin Way) had noted a spectacular increase in private admissions, including those requesting convalescent beds. £8 million had been received in NHS contracts and they were still taking patients from Portsmouth and Guildford. The hospital was free of debt following the sale of the Sherburne and the Hurst Park site, the projected deficit of £990,000 was less than anticipated, and she hoped for a small surplus next year. It was even possible to re-roof one wing at the cost of £800,000.

Then in January 2002, the linear accelerator used for deep radiotherapy failed, and 25 patients had to be switched to Guildford and Portsmouth. It was decided to replace this unit, but at an estimated cost of £5 million it was a major expense.

In February Lin Way reported that although most of the hospital was active and business was up 25%, costs were still disproportionately high. Up to 20 jobs were under threat, although these probably did not include nurses. Eventually four management posts were lost, including that of Director of Nursing and Quality, who was not replaced after her retirement.

In September, Lady Barttelot, who had supervised the Gertrude Jekyll gardens for 12 years, created a new area opposite the main entrance, planted with golden roses and plants with gold and silver foliage. The centenary of the laying of the Foundation Stone, together with the Queen's Jubilee, would be celebrated the next year, and it was hoped she would mark these occasions by a visit.

In November, Lin Way announced that the Hospital's future was secure. After nine months of discussion, a partnership had been formed with HCA International, owner of six large private hospitals and a major health care laboratory in London. They had signed a non-binding letter of intent, subject to a detailed review and discussion with the NHS, and hoped to complete by January. The Hospital charity would still own the building, but HCA would upgrade it, with an emphasis on cardiac, orthopaedic and cancer therapy. The radiotherapy facilities were a particular attraction, since these were in short supply nationally.

Provisional Liquidation

Then came disaster. At the end of December, the partnership deal collapsed and the Hospital faced imminent closure.

HCA had pulled out of the negotiations due to a 40% reduction in NHS support over the previous three months. The Health Authority had not taken up an option to provide a 70-bed orthopaedic unit to relieve waiting lists, and was spending £9 million on a diagnostic treatment centre in Chichester, duplicating that at Midhurst. While King Edward VII was giving radiotherapy to 1000 local patients a year, the new cancer centre, due for completion in May, would not be finished unless £5 million could be provided.

The local MP, Andrew Tyrie, wrote to the Health Minister, stressing the urgent need for capital support to prevent closure. The reduction in NHS support had left the Hospital with spare capacity despite there being long waiting lists elsewhere and a policy of sending patients abroad for treatment. Other MPs, both Conservative and Liberal Democrat, were supporting him and he raised the matter in Parliament.

A phased closure was due to start on 1st February, but a week before, the NHS committed itself to directing £900,000 of new business to Midhurst within two months; this being equivalent to 280 patients.

The Fight Back

The Provisional Liquidator, Shay Bannon, was an Irishman working for BDO Stoy Hayward, the fourth largest accounting firm in the world. Initially he thought he would be closing the Hospital quickly, but he reckoned without public support. A petition collected 80,000 signatures, Andrew Tyrie received 500 letters, £51,000 was collected for a fighting fund, a website was set up and three coach loads of staff lobbied Parliament. Even the Queen was informed.

A public meeting attended by nearly 600 people was told that the Hospital was losing £300,000 a month. Although many speakers blamed this on a sudden fall in NHS spending, a representative of the Health Care Trust denied they were solely to blame, and during the previous year they had paid £2 million for cardiac surgery. NHS spending fluctuated from year to year with the Hospital receiving between £4.9 million and £6.3 million.

A further problem was that the Hospital had lost its charitable status when it went into liquidation. Money already collected had been "ring fenced" but it was necessary to cancel two forthcoming fund raising events, the Spring Fair and the Sponsored Ride. Another charity, the Macmillan Unit was also in difficulty, Midhurst was at the centre of its catchment area, and it would be a real misfortune if it had to surrender the hospice ward.

Finding a Buyer

On 7th January 2003, the Financial Times carried an advertisement, offering the building for sale, and 40 organisations showed an interest. Then in March, Brian Atkins, the newly appointed chief executive announced a rescue plan, although there would be 30 immediate redundancies.

A consortium was wishing to buy the site, converting the hospital building into 382 residential units and erecting a new 120-bed, £30 million hospital, which would include the Macmillan unit. Four companies were involved, Capio, a Swedish firm who owned 21 acute hospitals across Europe and the UK; MIA Lodestone specialising in medical diagnostics, Lincoln Holdings, a property developer and YJL Construction, the builders.

The existing building was quite unsuitable for a 21st century hospital. It was very expensive to heat and wasteful of space (42% of the area was used for corridors, staircases and access instead of 18% as recommended) and porters walked three miles a day just taking patients to the Rehabilitation Centre. It was not even possible to use the balconies, as the railings did not meet modern safety standards.

Site plans included the provision of a safer junction between the access road, Kings Drive, and the A286, a heat exchange facility to generate electricity, and a "grey water" plant to reduce dependence on mains supplies. There would be a GP's surgery, a health club for residents, a village shop and a recycling point for household waste. Some land would go to the National Trust and the

Gertrude Jekyll gardens would be restored together with the measured walks. But some early ideas were shelved. There would be no care home, no warden-assisted site, and Chichester District Council would receive £3.65 million in lieu of building 48 affordable homes.

Originally it was hoped that Chichester District Council would rule on the planning application by June, but this was deferred until the autumn to allow a full environmental impact study. In addition British Nature and the Sussex Downs Conservancy Board asked for a report on wildlife in the area.

The plan alarmed the residents of Hurst Park who feared for their amenities and property values. Easebourne Parish Council voted to reject it, since it would increase the village's population by 50% and strain local services. However Midhurst Town Council gave it a cautious welcome since it would prevent widespread redundancy and go some way to meeting the Government's target for new housing. But meanwhile, the Hospital's centenary passed almost unnoticed.

Seeking Agreement

On 15th October a Chichester District Planning Committee agreed to the new development by a single vote, despite opposition from its own planners. Then on 5th November, the full council gave its backing to the proposal by 22 votes to 19.

The Government still had the right to order a full public enquiry. This could take 18 months, a delay which would be fatal to the plan, but John Prescott, the minister responsible, decided against this option since this was an exceptional case.

However there was one more, unexpected challenge; Tony Lawson, a Haslemere businessman, sought a judicial review of the planning consent and lodged £50,000 with his lawyers. He thought that the existing agreement was toothless, and feared that the housing development would go ahead without a new hospital being built. But ironically his action would delay the project and might well put it jeopardy.

In response, Capio explained that they were expecting a £250 million contract with the NHS, and had been assigned "preferred bidder status" to provide ten treatment centres across England. They hoped to sign a five-year contract for orthopaedic and general surgery at Midhurst by the spring, investing £18 million and delivering by 1st April 2005.

Nonetheless another clause was added to the planning application, insisting that the funds to build the new hospital were made available before house construction began, and that it would be fully operational before they were all occupied. The medical facilities would be used for a minimum of five years with at least 25% of the patients being NHS or publicly funded.

Despite this, Tony Lawson instructed his lawyers to be ready to proceed during the statutory 90-day period for legal challenges. He finally withdrew his opposition in July after consulting with top lawyers, although he intended to maintain a watching brief.

Fresh delays

Shay Bannon was now free to sell the hospital and grounds to Lincoln Holdings and complete the agreement with Capio. The revised plan called for 348 homes and a 134-bed hospital, with 15 for the Macmillan unit, a 60-bed neurological facility and the remainder shared between cardiac surgery, cardiology, cancer and orthopaedics. And although it would now be a commercial rather than a charitable venture, the Queen had no objection to it continuing to bear the name of her great grandfather.

But eight months later, in March 2005, the contracts had still not been signed, and the Hospital was facing a compulsory winding up order. Instead the High Court granted Mr. Bannon another seven months protection in which to complete the transaction. He now expected the handover to occur in November with the creditors being paid within six weeks, but by February 2006 he was still waiting.

The delay was also very demoralising for the staff, particularly as they had endured a pay freeze for three years. The building was deteriorating, one of the two boilers was out of action and when the steam steriliser was used all the heating had to be switched off for ten minutes. Neither the chapel nor the recreation hall could be used, and even the car park was in urgent need of resurfacing.

There had been some progress. In May 2005 Capio began running the Hospital and had installed an accounting system compatible with their other hospitals. They had directed some of their NHS patients to Midhurst and 60% of the work now came from that source. Lincoln Holdings had made financial arrangements to buy the site although there were still some unresolved matters. And despite the uncertainty, in December 2005 the Hospital won an award for excellence in cancer care, one of only 15 centres across Europe which the European Society for Medical Oncology honoured in this way.

Closure

The end came with brutal suddenness. On 9th March 2006, Shay Bannon announced that the Hospital would close within a fortnight, making 239 staff redundant. Capio had decided to withdraw from the consortium despite having spent £1.5 million on planning. They blamed this on a failure to resolve what they described as a very complex negotiation.

Mr. Bannon later told the Midhurst and Petworth Observer, "I feel gutted. I am so upset. We have put in so much work and effort. It gets under your skin this place. It has great healthcare provision and it goes against all principles to have to close it. It seems bizarre."

The clinical work wound down very quickly; the last operation was performed that evening, and the final patient discharged on the 16th of March. The hospital manager, Paul Duhig, told the paper "the alternative to a speedy shutdown was riskier. We could have got into a situation where we were not sure whether we could hold all the services together because key staff would begin to move out to other jobs."

The management immediately arranged for advisors to assist the staff find new positions and alternative accommodation for those living in the hospital. However it was a difficult time to find fresh employment, the NHS was suffering a funding crisis, and there were 4000 redundancies nationally during the month.

Another considerable task was rearranging hospital bookings. Outpatient clinics held in Midhurst, were rescheduled to St Richard's, and patients awaiting admission, were referred to other hospitals; in West Sussex alone there were about 80 such cases. The staff were inundated with queries, many from elderly people who dreaded going elsewhere for treatment. They also arranged cover for individuals undergoing long term monitoring, such as those with pacemakers.

A particular concern was for 200 cancer sufferers cared for by the Macmillan Unit. A few who were near death were transferred to the Community Hospital, while arrangements were made with the West Sussex Primary Care Trust to provide services, such as blood transfusions and chemotherapy in patients' homes. Fund raising would continue with several activities planned for the year, but it was extremely unlikely that they would be able to set up another hospice; since, while this was cost effective within a hospital, stand-alone units were unsustainably expensive.

The final Hospital function was on Friday 24th March. A message of regret was received from the Queen and buglers from HMS Nelson at Portsmouth played "Sunset" while the flag was lowered for the last time; then there was a farewell party for the staff. A few would be staying on to sort out hospital records and patient files, and to answer queries, but they would not be able to celebrate the centenary of the official opening on June 13th, less than three months later.

Sources
Large SE. "King Edward VII Hospital Midhurst, 1902-1986" (Phillimore, Chichester).
Mitchell W. Manuscript which carries the history forward from 1986.
Hunt J. "Midhurst and Petworth Observer".

7. Easebourne Primary School

Origins

Easebourne and South Ambersham Parochial Schools as Easebourne Primary School was originally known, opened on the 10th of January 1873 under the patronage of Henry, 6th Earl of Egmont. There were other village schools, West Lavington (1853) and Midhurst (1854) and Kelly's Directory refers to an Easebourne Village School for girls in 1862 run by Mrs. Mary Osborn and in 1866 by Mrs. Ann Stone but the present School was a product of the 1870 Education Act.

This stipulated that there should be a school place for every child who wanted it. Opportunity was given to Voluntary schools, mostly church foundations, to fill this need, and only where they failed, were rate-funded Board schools set up. An Education Committee provided overall supervision.

Easebourne was originally considered as two separate schools, infants (up to age of seven) and mixed (seven to twelve); housed in the same building but with their own head teachers. Between 1885 and 1912 the older children were divided into boys and girls' schools with separate heads, but then the three sections were combined, under one headmaster with infant, mixed junior and mixed senior departments. A plan of the school drawn in 1911 is included.

Finance

Unusually for a voluntary foundation, Easebourne school was non ecclesiastical, established under a Trust Deed by Lord Egmont of the Cowdray Estate. This established a Board of Managers to administer it, though it was under the chairmanship of the Vicar and there was a stipulation that all teachers should be members of the Church of England.

Lord Egmont and his successors funded the school building, and extensions made in 1880, 1885 and 1895. They also paid for major improvements, such as upgrading the heating and toilets and connection to the main drainage system in 1905. They even provided a merry-go-round for the children.

The Cowdray Estate continued to pay for major projects up to the 1930s. These included partitioning one of the rooms, repair of the playgrounds and installation of mains electricity in 1931.

Local ratepayers were asked to give a voluntary rate of about 2% in the pound and parents were also expected to pay for their children's education. In 1882 the head teacher called for the fees to be raised and the next year a scale was agreed. The first child in any family would be charged 2d a week, and each additional one 1d. However if the family did not pay the voluntary rate, each child was charged 2d.

A former pupil, J.Morley, remembered bringing his money on Monday mornings, but when he was appointed "school-something", which involved cutting wood and bringing in coal for fires and tidying up after lessons, he and his brother were educated free and he received 3d a week.

Parents paid a weekly fee for their children's tuition until legislation in 1891 provided more Government money. However the Guardians of the Midhurst Union Workhouse were less forthcoming. They had closed their own school in 1896 and transferred 13 children to Easebourne, but refused to pay for them until forced to do so by the Education Department.

The school was examined each year by Her Majesty's Inspector (HMI) and Government grants were given if the quality of teaching was deemed adequate, (the "payment by results" principle). There was also an annual Diocesan inspection to examine religious education, even although this was not a church school.

Local Education Authorities

The 1902 Education Act established Local Education Authorities (LEA). While providing a more secure financial base for the school, these reduced the powers of the Managers.

New legislation between 1904 and 1907 widened the curriculum, adding subjects such as cookery and gardening, encouraging the provision of school meals, and establishing routine medical examinations. And for the first time, academically gifted children could win scholarships to establishments such as the Midhurst Grammar School. But it was 1921 before the school leaving age was raised from 12 to 14 and only after the Second World War did it become 15.

End of the Estate School

The first Lord Cowdray had set up an Ecclesiastical Trust Fund, which paid £100 annually to the school. But in 1933 during the depths of the Depression, his son wrote to the Managers saying he had reluctantly decided to discontinue this, and suggested the school be handed over to the LEA as a county school.

The second Lord Cowdray died later that year, but his successor eventually agreed to pay £50 per annum so that the school could continue to operate in the voluntary sector. It was only in 1949 that it assumed controlled status, with the Cowdray Trust leasing the building and maintenance to the LEA.

World War II

For five years after World War I, the school educated London children who were being boarded out in the parish, but a far greater challenge was waiting.

On 1st September 1939, a mass evacuation began of school children from the large cities to the country. For Easebourne, the main influx was from London, the Johanna Street School close to Waterloo Station, although later some evacuees came from Portsmouth as coastal towns were bombed. There was also a contingent of 37 "Waifs and Strays" (now known as the Church of England Children's Society), boys up to the age of 14 who required discipline, and had been referred by Criminal Courts or expelled from other homes. Sadly the master in charge of them was later dismissed on sexual abuse charges.

In a few days the school roll tripled, although most of the children returned to London within a few months of the early part of the war, before air raids began. However in July 1945 there were still eight evacuees whose homes had been destroyed or whose parents could not be traced.

Although many teachers came with the children, this placed a huge burden on resources and a massive reorganisation was required. For the first year, pupils were taught on a half time basis, enjoying recreation for the rest of the day in the Village Institute. Staff took leave in rotation, and at Christmas 1939 a programme of entertainments was provided for the visitors.

In September 1940 the school was reorganised, with all the children integrated into two groups, the seniors being taught in the Institute and the juniors in the school building. However the situation was quite unsettled as new evacuees arrived and others left. It was also very difficult to get supply teachers and on one occasion the Headmaster was forced to teach 80 children at once!

Tragedy hit Petworth School on 9th September 1942 when a stray German bomb killed two teachers and 28 boys. Fortunately Easebourne was spared apart from one girl who suffered shock from a nearby explosion, and a V1 flying bomb, which passed harmlessly overhead.

Post War Reorganisation

In December 1945, Woolbeding School closed and all 31 pupils were relocated to Easebourne. In June 1947 a group of boys arrived from a hostel for first time offenders. Although one was described as a habitual pickpocket, they did not cause any major problems during their year as pupils at Easebourne. In 1951 the infants and juniors from Lodsworth School arrived when it too closed. But another big change had just occurred locally.

On 23rd May 1951, the new Midhurst Secondary Modern School was opened. All children aged 11 or above from the village schools went there, apart from those who had passed their 11 plus examination, the boys of whom attended the Grammar School and the girls Chichester High School. Easebourne was now a primary school.

Locally education became comprehensive in 1966, with the amalgamation of the Grammar and Secondary Modern Schools, but there was a further change four years later, with the opening of Midhurst Intermediate School. Now children left Easebourne at the age of ten to spend three years in the nearby school, before proceeding to the comprehensive Grammar School.

System of teaching

When Easebourne opened in 1873, the main emphasis was on the three "Rs" (Reading, wRiting and aRithmetic). During their time in school the more able pupils were expected to pass through seven grades known as "Standards", one per year.

The head teachers were registered by the Education Department as "duly certificated." Supporting them were qualified assistants, monitors and pupil teachers.

The monitorial system began in the early 19th century due to a dearth of trained teachers. Children, some as young as 13, supervised classes for which they were paid as little as one shilling a week (5p). They could then apply to become pupil teachers, undergoing a five-year apprenticeship. They received extra tuition and took yearly exams to become qualified assistants, and could then sit the Queen's Scholarship to qualify them for two years in a teacher training college, and the prospect of a senior post.

Monitors and pupil teachers were phased out early in the 20th century, but many staff trained by this method continued to work, for instance Miss Fanny Ford retired in 1937 after 41 years in the school.

Needlework and Cookery

Although many of the classes were mixed, girls and boys had their own specialised lessons.

Girls spent much time doing needlework, an essential skill before cheap manufactured clothing became available. But there were compensations, in the first few years of the school Lord Egmont gave them annual gifts of pinafores, underclothing and red cloaks, some of which they made themselves from materials he had supplied. In contrast the boys only received one or two shillings (5 or 10p) at Christmas for good attendance!

In 1910, a Mrs. C. S.Greenhill left £100 to provide two needlework prizes. However well intentioned, this led to the tendency for the girls to make garments to win awards rather than be of practical use. The prizes were discontinued in 1955 and the fund used to buy more needlework supplies.

Cookery lessons for the senior girls began in 1906, supported by a Government Grant. The Education Committee supplied a coal range, housed in what became the junior classroom.

Originally the Headmistress took the classes herself, to the detriment of discipline amongst her other pupils, but in 1909 a special instructress was appointed. Then in 1917 the range was declared unfit, and the lessons were transferred first to the Village Institute and then to the Refectory.

1928 saw the establishment of the Midhurst Domestic Subjects' Centre in the Congregational Church Hall on the corner of the Petersfield and Bepton Roads, under the direction of a Miss N. Smith. Girls from sixteen local schools attended weekly, with between six and fourteen coming from Easebourne.

They took a one or two year course, cooking with coal, oil, gas and electricity and learned how to produce economical and nourishing meals. They also practised laundry work, housewifery, needlework and childcare.

In September 1948, new handicraft rooms were opened at the school in "Horsa" prefabricated concrete huts. These had cooking facilities for 20 girls and were shared with other senior pupils from the neighbourhood, but when in 1951 the Secondary Modern School opened, all the equipment was moved there.

Gardening

In the Victorian period boys were given lessons in additional subjects such as geography and science and later drawing. Then in 1901, the County Council asked Easebourne to institute a practical Cottage Gardening Course for them, but it was five years before land became available and even then they had to move several times to different sites.

The Headmaster was supposed to be in charge, but due to pressure of work and illness there were frequent interruptions. In 1912 the course was abandoned altogether after an adverse report by HMI emphasising the unsuitability of the plot and the poor standard of tuition.

A new "grant earning" class began in February 1919 and four years later Mr. Silcock, the former head gardener at Hollycombe House joined the staff. During his 13 years with the school, the garden flourished despite problems with the weather and the periodic incursion of cows through a damaged fence. A profit was made on the sale of produce, and an annual award of a spade was made to the best pupil.

The course was still running in 1939 under the direction of the Headmaster though there is no record of when it finally closed. However in February 1977 there was another call for gardening instruction for the children and an appeal was made for tools.

Singing and Sport

Singing was an important part of the Victorian curriculum. It was examined during the annual inspection, contributing to the Government grant, and in addition the pupils would often perform for distinguished guests. Then in 1896 the first of a series of carol competitions was held, and the children began giving school concerts.

Singing lessons followed in 1913 for a selected group of children, and in April 1928 the school began competing in the Petersfield Choral Competition. This event proved so popular that for several years the school was closed on that day. A similar competition began in Midhurst in 1945 and the school again took an enthusiastic part.

The first mention of physical exercise was in 1888 when drill lessons, described as extension motions, began in the schoolyard since there was no room inside. Later the boys began dumbbell exercises.

Cricket prizes were awarded in 1909, and the 1911 school plan included a playing field for the boys. Ten years later they were competing in a Football Competition while the girls were also playing field games.

The early 1930s saw an interest in athletics with a school sports day and with inter-school competitions held both locally and at Chichester. Teams from the school also took part in a physical training display at Goodwood House, at a school exhibition, and at various agricultural shows.

Post-war activities showed an even wider range of sports, including tennis, netball and rounders, and matches were played against schools as far away as Bognor Regis. Swimming instruction began in 1958 at St. Cuthman's but it was 1964 before Easebourne had a pool of its own.

Evening Classes

Pupils who had left school were not forgotten. During the years 1889 to 1904 several attempts were made to establish an Evening Continuation School on the premises under the auspices of the County Council and with Government grants. Its most successful period was between 1897 and 1901.

In the first winter, the Headmaster taught reading and writing, geography, arithmetic, mensuration (measurement of lengths, areas and volumes) and drawing, at a cost of 3d per week on two nights. A separate instructor gave a course on shorthand at 6d. A summary made at the end of the course showed an average enrolment of nineteen for the six topics, with a 41% attendance.

Next winter only four subjects were taught including "the life and duties of a citizen" and geometrical drawing. Numbers continue to fall despite suggestions that a magic lantern should be used and that students be entered for NUT examinations.

By 1901 the Managers had incurred a debt of over £3, and since less than 20 students had applied they decided to close down. One final attempt to run classes two years later was abandoned as a fiasco.

Other Activities

The premises were also used for other events. In the 1870s there were penny readings; lectures on cruelty to animals and temperance, and later a magic lantern show on the colonies and talks on topics such as Submarine Cables and Wild Flowers. The Easebourne Penny Bank and the Band of Hope held entertainments there and it was hired out on a regular basis to the Sunday School, the Parish Council, the Fife and Drum Band and the Red Cross.

In 1926 a representative of the Gramophone Company gave a lecture on "Musical Appreciation" and the senior children heard talks on such diverse subjects as the League of Nations and "Dress through the Ages". By the 1950s the police were showing the children films on road safety.

Holidays

In the Victorian Period, farming was still labour intensive, and children were expected to help. The pupils were given three weeks off during the main harvest, though the day they broke up was only set at the last moment depending on the state of the crop; it varied between July 31st and August 23rd. Many families then went hop picking and it was several weeks into the autumn term before they all returned

Another week's holiday was given in October for the children to make money collecting sweet chestnuts from the long avenue north of the Priory. Opinions vary as to whether these were used to feed the deer which roamed the park, or to be sold in London. After Christmas many boys went "bird stopping", that is preventing pheasants escaping along hedgerows during a shoot.

The children also played their part during the World Wars. In 1918 the Board of Agriculture wrote regarding "the urgent necessity of increasing the supplies of jam for the Navy, Army and Civilians." On several afternoons the children went blackberrying and picked nearly 8½ hundredweight of fruit (about 430 kg).

In 1943, the summer holiday was cut from five to three weeks during which time many older children helped harvest the grain. Another fortnight was allowed at the end of September when assistance was needed with crops such as sugar beet.

Holidays were also given for Church Festivals. There was usually a fortnight's vacation at Christmas, a week at Easter and Whitsun, and a day off for Ash Wednesday and Ascension Day. In August there was usually a school treat, for instance in 1882 "242 children sat down to tea in the park, and a considerable number of friends were present." Half-holidays were also granted when circuses or other entertainments came to town.

National Events

An innovation in 1905 was the celebration of "Empire Day" on May 24th, a tradition which continued until the Second World War. Often this just involved singing the National Anthem and "O God our help in ages past", hearing a talk on Empire from a distinguished visitor and running up a flag on the school flagpole. In 1923 the Managers bought a gramophone record with a special message from King George V and in 1936 the whole school listened to a programme on the Wireless.

From 1928 onwards the pupils often joined other schools for a big ceremony at the Cowdray Ruins, which often included a school band, and a sports meeting or a walk on the South Downs afterwards. From 1919 the school also marked Armistice Day on November 11th with two minutes silence and a ceremony in the playground.

Absenteeism

Until 1877 school was voluntary, but then a School Attendance Board was set up with an officer who had power to enforce the children's presence.

Now that most people have access to a car, it is easy to forget how weather used to affect attendance. In the 19th century almost all children walked to school, some up to three miles each way, and few had weatherproof clothing so they were usually kept at home if there was rain or snow. In 1900 Lord Egmont gave 36 mackintoshes for those pupils who lived furthest from school, and in 1911, Lady Cowdray suggested supplying a conveyance for children coming from Ambersham and Henley, but it was nearly 30 years before buses were provided.

Illness was another problem, particularly before immunisation for most diseases was available. In April 1873 "measles raging fearfully throughout the parish and on Friday we had one hundred absentees almost exclusively on that account". Subsequently the school was closed for a week.

There were also periodic closures for outbreaks of mumps, scarlet fever, diphtheria, whooping cough, chickenpox and influenza. Individuals might also be excluded if suffering from ringworm or head lice. One boy was sent home after having five fits in one day while another such sufferer fell and "struck his head very violently on the Harmonium". The parents of a third boy wrote saying "that he would never come to school again as he is suffering from paralysis of the heart."

Truancy

Unauthorised absences were a major problem, particularly in the early days when the pattern of regular attendance was new. Mothers regularly removed their older daughters to help at home and truancy was rife during July when the wortleberries were ripe. Before ice creams and chocolates were readily available these wild fruits were irresistible.

Bird stopping continued unofficially, and it was said that the older pupils "make it a rule to come to school on Mondays and Fridays only". Winter was also the time to fell timber and many children went "chip picking".

Some pupils were regular truants. In 1902 the attendance officer was informed of "the very irregular way in which the Bexley Hill children attend school. One family... withdrew themselves from attending this school some three years ago and have not been since though still of school age."

But incentives were given for good attendance. Apart from monetary rewards at Christmas, the names of those with a perfect record were put up on boards or they might receive books, medals or even a watch.

Discipline

The school logs and a punishment book record some misdemeanours committed by the pupils. For instance in 1874, the Headmaster forbade bird's nesting and climbing trees "unless a note be brought from the parent to the effect that I am to send for a Doctor in case of a fall, or a conveyance to take them to their homes."

Girls might be given extra work or sent home, but this was not always popular. In 1874 one mother arrived "in a bundle of threats, abuse and insults and with open confession that 'she has instructed her children in no way to be trampled upon by the teachers.'"

Boys often received corporal punishment although they did not always accept it without a fight. Some were excluded and only allowed to return after an appeal from their parents and having made an apology in front of the whole school.

In 1917 some boys threw stones and sticks at a new teacher and "tried to upset her off her bicycle by putting pieces of stick inside the wheels". She resigned after one day, and since the culprits could not be identified, all privileges were forfeited for a year. Eight years later, four boys assaulted a girl on her way home, and to the annoyance of the Managers, a report was given to the Attendance Officer and the Rescue Lady from Haslemere.

Cigarettes were also a problem. In 1912 it was claimed that 20 pupils were smoking and a local shopkeeper was asked to stop serving them. But sympathy should be felt for the workhouse boy who was caught writing notes to one of the girls. He was warned "that if it ever occurred again he would be severely punished!"

Headteachers

The original headmaster, Alexander Foard was chosen on November 9th 1872. This was almost a family appointment since his wife Sarah became the sewing mistress and daughters Caroline and Alice were made monitors.

Mrs. Foard seems to have been conscientious since she only took one month off to have another baby but in 1877 she had a problem with the Managers. No reason was stated but it gave the Foards "Domestic Affliction" and led to their resignation.

Their successors Samuel and Elizabeth Moore were mediocre and the reports of the annual Government inspections were disappointing. In 1884 the Managers decided that "the school was losing ground," and gave them six months notice, but they were still there next summer and now there was a further problem.

Teachers were sometimes given discretion to withdraw a child with severe learning difficulties from the inspection to avoid a spurious result, but Mr. Moore excluded 16! Moreover 23 others were repeating work from the year before and the arithmetic results were so poor that HMI could not recommend any merit grant. The school had lost a considerable part of its funding.

Mr. Moore resigned on the 18th of July aged 61, and when the position was advertised there were 55 replies. In October Mr. George Singleton from Wiltshire was engaged at a salary of £50, bonuses and accommodation while his wife Ruth received £40 as head of the infants.

For most of his 27 years as head, the schools flourished. Although the annual inspectors' report of 1888 found some weaknesses, they stated "the general improvement upon last year's work under the new Master reflects high credit upon him...the discipline has already become very satisfactory. I have pleasure in recommending the good merit grant on account of the improvement..."

J. Morley remembered both his strictness and his kindness. After a stormy autumn night, he and his brother picked up so many chestnuts from the Avenue that they filled their pockets and school bags and even threw away their packed lunches to make more space.

Arriving late at school Mr. Singleton called them over and confiscated all their chestnuts though they did not get the expected caning. But at lunchtime they were invited to the School House where they enjoyed a hot dinner, the only one he had during his school days.

Another pupil, May Carver was less fortunate. She too threw away her packed lunch to make room for chestnuts, only to have them taken away and she had to face a very hungry afternoon.

In 1894 when Miss Annie Crump resigned as head of the girls' school to get married, Mrs. Singleton was employed at a salary of £76, though she had to take "temporary retirement" at the end of the year due to poor health.

In 1902 the Managers gave them a bonus "in recognition of their continued devotion to the interests of the schools." Later that year Mr. Singleton won a county council scholarship for an 18-day course on "Nature Study" at Cambridge with the Managers refunding his out-of-pocket expenses. But there were problems ahead.

George Soane who was a pupil between 1895 and 1902 recalled that "On Fridays big boys were sent to Midhurst to do shopping for Mr. and Mrs. Singleton, this involved a large wicker basket which was fully packed- all boys being aware that a bottle of spirits was at the bottom as arranged with the grocer. Boys were instructed to walk through the Park Gate and keep to the path via Cowdray Ruins and arrive in North Street. In this way they avoided Miss Osborne, the most important Manager, who lived on the normal route into the Town and was to be avoided at all costs. Boys rather enjoyed this half day from school."

This subterfuge could not last indefinitely. In March 1911 the Managers noted that they "have had under consideration certain complaints with regard to the lack of discipline in the School, the sending of boys on errands, and their employment for other purposes than intended during school hours." In addition they asked that "the chairman be requested to see Mr. Singleton with regard to the lack of discipline in the School and matters affecting his conduct as Head Teacher."

In December, while he was away suffering from an internal haemorrhage the Managers convened a special meeting to discuss "the causes of Mr. Singleton's illness and of his repeated inability to be in charge of the schools."

Later that day they decided to ask for his resignation and sent him a registered letter. At the same time they received a request from him for three months sick leave.

Unfortunately there were irregularities in the way the meeting was called, so two days later they reconvened and passed a fresh resolution to the same effect "he not having kept the pledge of total abstinence taken by him on March 26th last and having reverted to intemperate habits thereby bringing the school into disrepute and seriously interfering with the proper performance of his duties, and that the Managers instructions conveyed to him by letter dated 22nd March respecting the sending of boys on errands during school hours having been disregarded."

After some dispute he agreed to go, but while working out his notice he had a brain tumour removed in the Chichester Infirmary. His wife meanwhile had retained her post, but her health was poor and she died that September.

There was one final twist to the story. A year later The Board of Education wrote to the school asking the reason for his resignation. Was he ill or did he have a drink problem and could his brain tumour have contributed to this? He had applied for a pension, but the Board's final decision was not recorded.

The Managers' first choice as Mr. Singleton's successor was rejected by the Board of Education and during the summer of 1912, six different supply teachers took charge. Then in September Frank Woodman became headmaster of the newly combined school. Later his wife Gertrude applied unsuccessfully for a fulltime post although she frequently acted as a supply teacher.

Mr. Woodman's rapport with his junior staff was poor, and in 1916, three assistant teachers wrote to the Managers accusing him of undermining their attempts at discipline, belittling them in front of the children, of constant interference amounting to tyranny and of unpunctuality.

Faced with increasing staff unrest and poor discipline, the Managers asked the Education Authority to transfer him to another school, but they deferred any action until after the war. In the event, despite further incidents he was still in post in 1927 at the age of 60.

That January the Managers again applied to the Education Committee for his removal. It refused since he still needed three years work to complete his pension and there was the threat of legal action by the NUT. However he resigned later that year and was replaced by the 27 year old William Bevan.

He held the post for 33 years, and unlike his predecessors was liked by both staff and managers and earned considerable respect outside the school. In 1936 he was the President of the County Association of Teachers.

His wife Mary, occasionally acted as a supply teacher, and in 1938 took charge of the school for three months while he was attending a course in Oxford. Then in November 1939 the LEA confirmed her as a certified teacher for the duration of the war. The pressures must have been immense, and once more in 1942 she took charge of the school for ten weeks while her husband was on sick leave. She herself was away for six weeks the next year.

Despite the temporary nature of her appointment, she was still on the permanent staff in 1951, and in 1956 even became deputy head, a post she held till her retirement four years later. William Bevan himself retired three months after her, and the new Headmaster Mr. Cuthbert Boole, (always known as Gus) took over at the beginning of 1961.

Unfortunately there must have been resentment among some assistant teachers about Mrs. Bevan's position, since they wrote to the Managers asking that the wife of the new Headmaster should not be employed in the same school as him.

This request was ignored and Mrs. Boole was appointed as an assistant teacher. Immediately staff relationships worsened, particularly with two teachers who began working to rule. Eventually the Director of Education had to transfer them to other schools.

Sadly Mrs. Boole died three years later but Mr. Boole became a very popular Headmaster. He retired in the Spring term of 1976 and two months later remarried. He served for a time as a Governor of Midhurst Intermediate School and passed away in April 1985.

The first major redevelopment for nearly 60 years occurred during his tenure. The work was planned in 1960 but was delayed for three years due to a national policy. An extension was built comprising an assembly hall and various other rooms. The external lavatories and a temporary classroom were demolished in order to give access to the playing field, which had been established in 1961.

Mr. Graham Lilley, Gus Boole's successor was 35 and came from Stoke on Trent. In 1977 he co-ordinated the building of a three foot deep swimming pool to mark the Queen's Silver Jubilee. Over half the estimated £8000 cost was saved by the use of volunteer labour and it was available to any local child of 13 or less, whether or not they attended the school.

In January 1989 work began on setting up an environmental site in the school grounds. The aim was to encourage various areas such as a wildflower meadow, wooded areas, wet and marshy places, a garden, a rockery and a paved section where the children could work. The Cowdray Estate loaned a digger and driver to make a trench for a boundary hedge and start excavating a pond, but the children and parents did much of the work.

Mr. Lilley resigned after 18 years and his successor was Mr. Steve Calvert who was appointed in January 1995. Sadly he died in September the next year and Mr. Arthur Bain took over in January 1997.

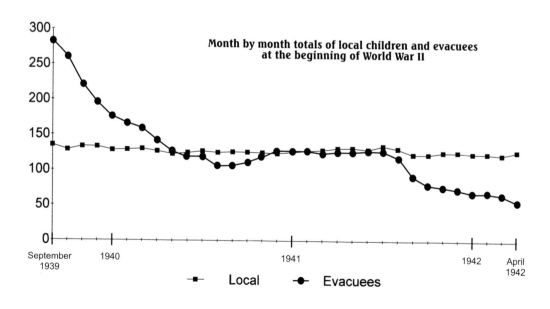

Month by month totals of local children and evacuees at the beginning of World War II

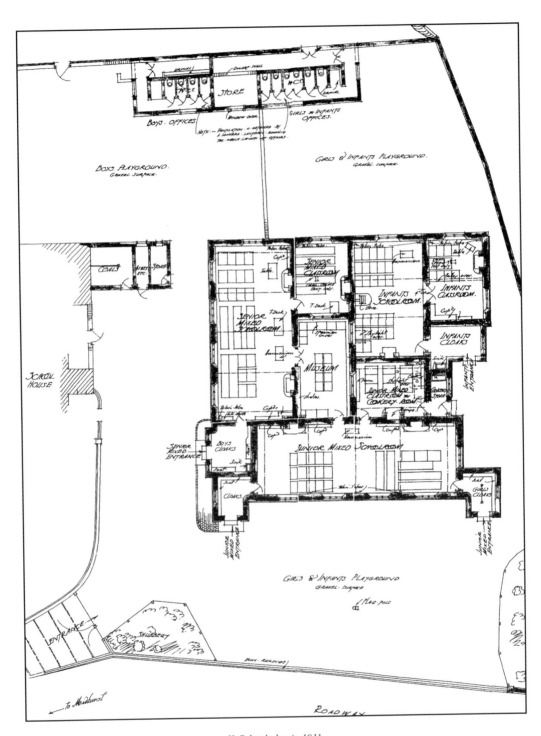

X. School plan in 1911.

7.1   The rural location is evident, as is the school house, on the left. It was usually occupied by the headmaster and his wife.

7.2   The main buildings at the hub of the school remain little changed, the local sandstone and brick quoins standing the test of time.

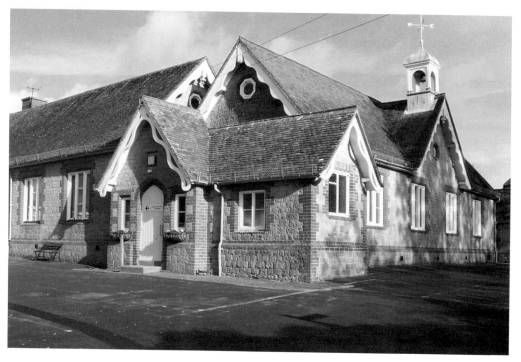

8. Midhurst Intermediate School

Why Midhurst Intermediate?

Despite its name, Midhurst Intermediate School (MIS) is situated in the parish of Easebourne. It is also somewhat unusual in that it takes children during the middle years of their schooling.

It opened on September 8th 1970 as a result of the formation of a three-tier system of education in the Midhurst area. Previously children had left their primary schools at the age of 11 to enter the newly comprehensive Midhurst Grammar School. Now they went to MIS at 10, and only on to the Grammar School when they were 13.

Most MIS pupils came from 12 primary or "feeder" schools. These comprised Camelsdale, Cocking, Easebourne, Elsted, Fernhurst, Harting, Hollycombe, Midhurst, Milland and Rake, Rogate, Stedham and West Lavington. These were all Victorian in origin apart from Harting (founded in 1834) and Camelsdale (1904).

In its first year, MIS took children aged 10-12 from the primary schools, but subsequently just those of 10 or 11. The roll rose from 417 in 1970 when there were only two separate year groups to 627 in 1971 with three. The first cohort of 13 year olds left for the Grammar School in 1972. The school is able to provide specialist teaching to Year 6, a year earlier than most other schools.

Links with Primary Schools

Strong links were maintained with the feeder schools. Their head teachers had lunch meetings at MIS and joined in study days, discussing topics such as the core curriculum or the teaching of French and Mathematics.

In 1971, 10 year-old primary pupils were invited to lunch to meet former classmates who had entered MIS the year before. These latter pupils in turn had lunch with their previous head teachers, and attended the combined primary school sports day and music festival.

In 1979 a new tradition began with an annual combined "potted sports" day at MIS. This was for the older primary pupils, and helped accustom them to their future surroundings. Up to 400 children attended and they were organised and coached by the senior MIS pupils. The school also provided a venue for other primary school events, such as a netball rally and an exhibition celebrating 900 years of Chichester Cathedral.

Parents of prospective pupils often visited MIS, and in 1976 the Head held meetings in all the feeder schools. The New Education Act of 1980 made this liaison more urgent since it gave parents greater freedom in choosing their children's school. Those living in Camelsdale and Fernhurst often preferred education in Surrey, and special meetings were held for them promoting MIS and Midhurst Grammar School.

Pupils with special needs were not forgotten either. Those with learning difficulties were assessed before entry so they could be given appropriate support. In 1989 the requirements of a wheelchair bound child from Camelsdale were discussed, and in 1991 a blind girl was transferred from West Lavington.

The school today is the heart of the Rother Valley School network and there are very strong links between our schools, with regular monthly meetings of Headteachers, and with teachers and pupils working together.

In 2006 the school became fully accessible to any child or adult with a disability.

Secondary schools

MIS kept close contacts with other local secondary schools. In October 1970 the Head held his first meeting with his opposite numbers from Midhurst Grammar and Herbert Shiner. The latter, sited in Petworth was another middle school whose pupils progressed to Midhurst Grammar.

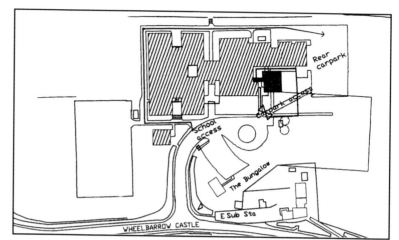

8.1 *Plan of the school in 1970. The rectangle on the left would become the site of the technology block.*

8.2 *A new road had to be cut into the hillside before work could start.*

8.3 *The school keeps at the forefront of technology and the exceptional warm relationship between staff members has meant some retired teachers continuing as volunteers.*

In March 1972 MIS hosted an Inter Schools Conference for staff from the three establishments, with a particular emphasis on the transfer of pupils at the age of 13. But perhaps the most imaginative approach was when six Grammar School pupils returned to MIS to talk to third year pupils and answer their questions just prior to their transfer.

In 2007 there was regular liaison between Midhurst Intermediate School, Herbert Shiner School and Midhurst Grammar School.

Heads

The first headmaster was Mr. C. R. Gillings. He was much in demand outside the school, being invited by the Secretary of State to serve on a Committee of Inquiry into the teaching of reading and use of the English language, and he also lectured in Malta on a British Council Teacher Vacation Course. He resigned in 1973 on being appointed a school inspector.

His successor, Mr. Mark Caton, had a very firm attitude towards discipline, once withdrawing all the children's privileges for five weeks following some unacceptable behaviour. In 1980 he took leave of absence for a year to study for a Master's Degree in Education at Southampton, with his deputy Mr. P. T. Neil acting as head. But instead of returning to the school, he became an advisor for middle and primary schools in West Sussex, and then a school inspector in Birmingham.

Mr. Neil successfully applied for the vacant post. In 1986 he followed Mr. Caton's example of studying for a Master's degree at Southampton, leaving the school in the hands of his deputy, Mr. John Wignall.

He took early retirement in 1991. This may have been prompted by the introduction of the National Curriculum and Local Management of Schools (LMS), which produced a major upheaval in education. His successor was Mr. Simon Davies, former deputy head at another intermediate school, Rydon Community College and he was followed in September 2006 by the appointment of Mrs Christine Denne.

Governors

When the school opened in 1970 there were 12 Governors. The chairman Mr. J. Lakin (Lord Cowdray's brother-in-law) served for 11 years, and the Board also included the vicar and a local GP. It was reconstituted in 1982 as the result of new legislation, and had eight elected members including two parent governors, two staff members and one minor authority representative, together with four co-opted ones.

During the 1980s the Governors' workload increased steadily, particularly with the financial stringencies of the time and changes in policy that made them more accountable. This made it difficult to recruit new members and in one election for a parent governor in 1986 there was only one nomination.

In 1988 the Board was again reconstituted, with four instead of two parent governors. They now had the responsibility of producing a school development plan in preparation for LMS. Inevitably this led to long meetings; at one there were 21 separate items on the agenda!

But despite all this hard work, the introduction of LMS in April 1990 was delayed by the failure of the authorities to provide current financial information, or even to tell the school their budget share! There was still uncertainty a year later.

The Governing Body in 2007 is a strong group that helps shape the future of the school. Their responsibilities continue to grow and develop.

The Site

The school was built on a 16½-acre, (6.7 hectare), site off the road named Wheelbarrow Castle. It included a library, language laboratory, open plan and single unit science laboratories, home studies facilities and art and craft areas. There was also a gymnasium, tennis and netball courts and extensive playing fields.

However not everything was ready when the school opened and it was two years before the playing fields could be used! The planners had also underestimated pupil numbers and within a month Mr. Gillings was discussing extension plans. When the full number of pupils arrived in 1971, there were insufficient venues available, so fewer classes could be taught and their size was increased. The new extension was opened in May 1973, but three years later further internal modifications had to be made to increase class space and improve circulation routes within the building.

There were various maintenance problems, particularly with the heating. The building was thin walled and badly insulated, a situation exacerbated when strict Government limits on fuel consumption were imposed in 1973 and 1979. Then, after only six years use, the main boiler had to be replaced providing an unexpected holiday for the pupils.

The system ducted hot air into each room, and by 1980 this was creating a severe dust hazard. Attempts were made to improve the situation using several different types of filter, but none proved effective and eventually a new gas-fired, water filled system was installed.

The hot water supply suffered from poor equipment and faulty installation and it often failed. On one occasion, a malfunction led to the unauthorised intervention by trade union representatives on behalf of the kitchen staff!

Initially the ground adjacent to the rear of the building was not paved or drained properly. In 1981 this caused seepage under the gymnasium floor, which then buckled. Other water damage in 1986 resulted from the failure of temporary roof coverings during a wet bank holiday and caused major problems with the ceilings.

The school was also a tempting target for intruders. Between 1977 and 1991 there were 12 break-ins and one theft of heating oil, though fortunately most losses were small, and the caretaker's dog disrupted one burglary!

The school only suffered minor damage during the great storms of October 1987 and January 1990. But its most worrying moment was in 1975 when a bomb was brought into the building buried in a bucket of earth! Fortunately it only proved to be a two-pound mortar smoke bomb, although the charge was still live.

A new Design & Technology block was built in 1997, new Science Laboratories were opened in 1999 and a new purpose-built Music Suite was built in 2002. The school continues to develop the facilities to support the pupils' learning.

Falling Roll

But a much more serious problem was the fall in the school roll. After the initial rise in 1971, numbers peaked at 684 in 1975, then fell steadily during the early 1980s to 385 in 1985, (a 43% decrease). During this time two of the feeder schools closed, Cocking in 1984 and Elsted in 1985.

The one advantage of this decline was that there was more space; in fact one classroom was "mothballed". But it meant that fewer staff could be employed.

In 1971 there were 31 teachers including the Headmaster, but by 1985 this had fallen to 20. Although there were some part time staff, it was more difficult to provide for specialised subjects or cover for absences. The academic year 1983-4 was particularly difficult since five teachers were hospitalised during that period.

It was also necessary to reduce the support staff particularly in the school kitchen. The post of canteen manageress was abolished in 1980.

The number of pupils in the school continues to fluctuate in response to the changes in the birth rate.

Promotion Problems

Problems also arose with the promotion prospects of teachers. These were employed on a series of scales, being rewarded for good work by elevation to a higher one at an enhanced salary. The number of such promotions per year was dictated by a points system, and in May 1975 MIS discovered they had been awarded the minimum quota, half that of a corresponding senior secondary school.

This severely upset morale, particularly among the junior staff who had less chance of achieving a higher grade, and it also impaired recruitment. Another problem was the cost of accommodation, one probationer teacher resigned because he could not afford to live in the area.

The Governors conducted a strenuous campaign to get more points. The County Education Committee appeared sympathetic, and by 1979 there seemed a realistic chance of improvement. But then a change of Government led to a large reduction in public expenditure and a period of austerity in education.

Cutbacks

The problem was highlighted in 1981 when at a meeting of the West Sussex Secondary Schoolteachers a cutback of £750,000 was discussed with the loss of 300 teachers countywide. This seemed particularly unfair since West Sussex had the lowest per capita expenditure of any of the 104 local authorities.

A special meeting of the Heads' Association reviewed the matter, although by now the projected cutback was only £200,000. Nevertheless expenditure was restricted for several years and staff still had poor promotion prospects.

Teaching unions reacted by calling for the withdrawal of goodwill so that staff would no longer supervise lunchtimes or undertake extra curricular activities. In April 1984 an afternoon strike left the Head teaching over 100 children at once, and later the first year pupils missed a day of school. However during a further dispute in 1985 the staff resisted pressure from their union and continued to work normally.

The Education Reform Act of 1988, which set up LMS, promised schools increased freedom in managing their own affairs and more control over their finances. However tight budget controls continued to make it difficult to employ fresh staff or improve the salaries of the existing ones.

Transport

MIS shared its buses with the Grammar School. However the younger pupils had to wait while the others were transported first, so that their school day started and ended later. The Governors tried unsuccessfully to rearrange the timetable in 1977, and in 1984 a 9 a.m. to 3.45 p.m. school day was suggested, but when a new bus schedule was introduced, the pupils still had to wait till 4.10 p.m. to leave.

An unexpected opportunity to experiment with an earlier day came in 1985. A dispute with the teaching unions meant that the Grammar School had to close at 2 p.m. making the buses available sooner. For the duration of the dispute the MIS lunch break was reduced to 40 minutes allowing the children to go at 3.30 p.m. But the adoption of the present "continental day" with an early start and finish was only introduced in the 1990s.

The way in which children were transported was discussed in 1981 when the County Council discontinued two bus routes saving £23,000 a year. The remaining vehicles were overloaded, but they were permitted to carry three children per seat!

Midhurst Intermediate School Association (MISA)

The school enjoyed a very good relationship with parents, some of whom volunteered to decorate rooms and give donations. But their most practical assistance was through the Midhurst Intermediate School Association (MISA). The first event was in 1973 when a ploughman's supper was held, but it was the next year before it was formally inaugurated.

As a fundraising organisation it was vital, planning such events as the Christmas and Summer Fairs, film evenings, barn dances, beetle drives and bingo. It paid most of the cost of a print room, provided stage curtains, sponsored drama performances, and purchased a video camera, computers and sports equipment including a cricket net. But its biggest commitment was to a minibus.

In 1978 a 30-seater vehicle was obtained from the ICI plant protection unit at Fernhurst, providing a considerable saving on school trips. Its existence was threatened three years later when the County Transport Officer suggested scrapping any vehicle over 12 years old and a fund was set up to buy a newer one. However it was only disposed of in 1990, when it became obligatory for drivers to have a public service vehicle licence, and a 15-seat replacement was obtained.

MISA continues to be very active in raising funds to support the school. In 2006 a replacement minibus was provided by the committee. This is extensively used by Midhurst Intermediate School and is also loaned to other schools in the Rother Valley.

School Trips

Educational visits were often made on "Standstill Days" when there was no schoolwork. A favourite destination was London; in particular the museums, while local venues included the Roman Palace at Fishbourne, Butser Hill Iron Age Farm and the Open Air Museum at Singleton, (now the Weald and Downland Museum).

Studies of the natural world were made at Kingley Vale, with its ancient yew forest and the Arundel Wild-Life Centre, while other interests were catered for by the Beaulieu Motor Museum and the Mechanical Music Museum in Chichester. Agriculture was not forgotten either with several visits to the South of England Show at Ardingly.

Some special trips were arranged to places such as Chichester Fire Station, a Chinese Exhibition in London and the Doomsday Exhibition in Winchester. But the most practical excursion was in 1982 when the school had a treasure hunt in Easebourne and brought back several bags of litter!

School trips remain an important educational element with trips to the theatre, the Royal Albert Hall and other venues.

Extracurricular Activities

In November 1972 it was decided to start a youth club for the senior pupils on Thursday evenings (later Wednesdays), run by staff volunteers. They hoped to gain recognition from the County Youth Committee, but since no member was over 13 it did not qualify as an official youth club and it was difficult to remunerate the workers.

The pupils were also too young to enrol in the Duke of Edinburgh Award scheme. Instead a similar Midhurst Intermediate School Award Scheme was launched in 1985. Activities included orienteering in the Queen Elizabeth Country Park.

In 2006 the school was described as having a 'dizzying array' of after-school activities on offer to pupils, with music and sport clubs arranged each day. A more recent feature of the school is the annual Activities Week which is held in July. All pupils are taken off timetable in order to experience and enjoy alternative activities not normally provided during the school day.

French Trips

In June 1973, 33 children enjoyed an eight-day holiday in France, and a similar trip was made the next year. Soon there were day excursions to Boulogne and Dieppe and short breaks in Normandy. Then in December 1976 plans were made to set up exchange visits with a school in Chartres.

These began six months later, with parties from the two localities spending time simultaneously in each other's countries. During their stay the French children were taken to Chichester and London.

It became an annual event; for instance in 1980 53 French pupils and 4 staff came from Chartres and Nogent Le Rotrou, Midhurst's twin town. In subsequent years MIS concentrated on Nogent Le Rotrou with the Chartres children going to Bohunt School in Liphook.

The two parties arrived at different times of year so that the children could live in each other's homes and get to know each other. Normally at least 30 English pupils were involved, although in 1986 there were only 16.

A typical exchange was in April 1988. Members of Midhurst Town Council addressed the 56 visitors in French, while they in turn presented MIS with a framed antique map of the Nogent region. On the last day of term they joined MIS pupils "in some rather boisterous games", and during the Easter holiday enjoyed a boat trip up the Thames, and visiting Buckingham Palace and St Paul's. But only 25 English pupils made the return visit in June.

The next year was the tenth anniversary of the Nogent Le Rotrou exchanges and three rose bushes were planted to mark the occasion. Then in 1990 MIS was presented with an engraved marble plaque.

The French Exchange continues to flourish.

Other holidays

In the early 1970s skiing trips were made to Austria but it was ten years before these were resumed. Over the years 1977-84 there was a vogue for pony trekking in mid Wales and 1982 saw the start of camping trips. These were mostly in Dorset, although the first year pupils spent one night on the school field.

There were walks along the South Downs Way, three groups of pupils went on a sailing course and there were two trips to the Norfolk Broads. Holidays were also arranged in the Lake District and Scotland, but strangely only one visit was recorded to the Isle of Wight. There were also three-day stays in London and weekend trips to activity centres in Herefordshire and Shropshire.

Entertainments

Outings were organised to London to see entertainment such as the Harlem Globetrotters and the Wembley Ice Show and shows such as "Cats", "Me and My Girl" and "Starlight Express". Local excursions included performances of everything from "MacBeth" to "The Lion, the Witch and the Wardrobe." There were also visits to the Grammar School to see their productions.

A number of theatre groups came into school, such as the Connaught, the Rainbow and the Pimlico. Musical items included American High School choirs and bands from Oregon, Milwaukee and Texas; there were two Brass Ensembles, some folk singers and the Ballet Rambert.

The school was host to activities ranging from a three-day book fair to a weekend workshop of dance. There were visits from television chefs and authors and talks on everything from the Mary Rose project to the experiences of a steeplejack. Nonhuman visitors included police horses, an ewe with two lambs, performing owls and a python.

Visitors

MIS had some distinguished visitors such as Lavinia, Duchess of Norfolk who attended an assembly to receive a cheque for the Prince of Wales' Jubilee Appeal. Mr. Hooley, the chief executive of West Sussex County Council also inspected the school since he was very interested in its philosophy, organisation and ethos. Sir Alec Rose who sailed single-handed around the world and Major General Frost of a "Bridge too Far" fame gave talks and other notables included a senior advisor of the British Council and an American sex therapist!

The school also attracted many teachers from overseas. In its first four years there were students and staff from Canada, Chile, Germany, the Netherlands, Norway, South Africa and the USA. In 1981 a party of 12 Vietnamese refugees (boat people), visited the school and made such an impression that they were invited back twice. Other guests included four Portuguese teachers, two Zulu nuns, ten Japanese and three Malaysian students. On one day in 1979 there were representatives of the Philippines, Sri Lanka, Bangladesh and India.

In January 1981 representatives of Gideon International gave New Testaments to all the children and staff, returning each year to make presentations to the new pupils. Another annual visitor was the school photographer whose visits provoked comments such as "it's amazing how quickly he works - very little fuss" and he "paralysed the school for the morning,"

In February 1978, a team from Southern TV (BBC) filmed children decorating eggs for a competition sponsored by Mr. Barnes - a parent egg farmer. From a total of 4000 eggs submitted from the southern region, three from MIS reached the final, gaining two second prizes and a highly commended!

In 1979 an ICI crew filmed the second year pupils enacting a scene in the Magistrates' Court as part of their course on law and order. Although they were rather cramped it was considered a great success. In subsequent years the event was re-enacted in school with guests including magistrates, police, solicitors, probation officers, social workers and shopkeepers. In 1984 the pupils even played out a "shop lifting" scene first.

Dr. John Fines of Bishop Otter, (teacher training) College visited several times to investigate learning skills. In 1991 Professor Henry Layn spent a day with pupils who were studying Saxon England; he was accompanied by his wife, Dr Fines, a history co-ordinator and a reporter from the

Times Educational Supplement.

During the Gulf war in 1991, the pupils wrote letters to men serving on HMS Gloucester. One respondent, leading seaman Philip Duckworth, later made two visits to the school, talking about his experiences and showing his kit and emergency equipment. The children treated him as a celebrity.

Care in the Community

Humanitarian causes were not neglected either. There were talks about the Royal Naval Lifeboat Association, Barnardos and the NSPCC, the experiences of a blind man, missionary work in Pakistan and Tearfund, a Christian relief organisation working in the Third World.

In 1983, some third year pupils visited four establishments for the mentally handicapped and were invited back for a Christmas concert where they raised £25 for the funds. Next month they entertained over 100 senior citizens and some residents from the handicapped centres. The school log noted that "the care, compassion and concern" shown by the youngsters "do them great credit". Further visits were made in the next two years to the Care Village at Petworth for adults with mental handicaps.

On several years before Christmas, vocal and instrumental groups from the school entertained elderly people. MISA invited these into school for social events and they were given produce donated for the Harvest Thanksgiving services.

There were several collections for good causes. A favourite method was the "Mufti Day" when pupils were "fined" for coming to school in their own clothes. Sometimes the children themselves organised their own raffles and discos. Popular causes were "Save the Children", "NSPCC" and "Children in Need". Overseas causes were not forgotten either with "Comic Relief" and specific collections for Africa, Nepal, Romania, Vietnam and Afghanistan. There were even fun runs to assist the British Olympic team in 1984 and 1988.

Supporting others in the community is an important aspect within the school. The pupils and staff choose to support a number of charities each term and hold termly events, such as non-uniform days or cake sales, to raise funds.

Postscript

By 2002, the Midhurst, Petworth and Storrington areas were almost the only parts of West Sussex still operating a three-tier system of education. When the Office for Standards in Education (OFSTED) inspected the Local Education Authority (in 2001) it recommended that they look at the different ages of transfer across the county and ascertain if this was affecting standards in schools. West Sussex County Council circulated a questionnaire among interested parties in the area. It explained the proposed changes, assessed the impact on the schools and asked for their opinion.

The Midhurst and Petworth Observer of September 26th contained an interview with the heads of MIS and Herbert Shiner, Simon Davies and Mike Mattinson. They supported the current system, citing the benefit of a gradual progression from primary, through middle to secondary school, and noted that Ofsted itself had reported a lack of progress in the early years of secondary education under the two-tier system.

Bill Benge, head of the Grammar School, replied the following week. He noted that the Government's education strategy was planned round the two-tier system with transfer at eleven. The three-tier approach produced various difficulties, including a distortion of the statutory assessment of pupils at eleven and fourteen, since in both cases this was mostly based on work done before they had transferred.

Most respondents to the questionnaire favoured maintaining the status quo. The Task Force set up by the County Council agreed and reprieved the middle schools. However they stressed the importance of improving communication, raising standards and developing strategies to deal with further falls in pupil numbers.

9. Trades and Occupations

Kelly's Directories

One source of information on occupations and trade in Easebourne during the latter half of the 19th and beginning of the 20th centuries, is Kelly's Directories. Between 1845 and 1938 they had a section on Easebourne, updated every few years, including the names and occupations of tradesmen. However these entries do not include the addresses, in fact even the locations are only indicated in a minority of cases.

Craftsmen

The nineteenth century was still dominated by the horse, and the directories list one smith and three blacksmiths. Wagons and carts were manufactured locally and there were three wheelwrights, (one was working as late as 1930) and a coachbuilder. However the internal combustion engine was taking over by the end of the period, as shown by entries for a motor garage and car hire facilities. There were also two market gardeners and, with the opening of the King Edward VII Sanatorium, two engineers.

In these years before mass produced footwear, there were four boot and shoemakers, including ones at Henley and Bexley Hill respectively. John (or Harry) Andrews was employed for 40 years at the Union Workhouse, where when need arose, he would shave and cut the hair of inmates, or supervise them overnight. He was last listed in Kelly in 1922, but actually retired seven years later.

Some trades have continued to the present. The four carpenters continued to find plenty of work locally, as did the two builders and the builders' merchant.

James Damer	Blacksmith	1851-66
William Hurst	Blacksmith	1882-98
Harry Soane	Blacksmith (Lutener Rd.)	1890-95
John Cranstone	Smith	1845-52
Mrs W. A. Etherington	Builder	1924-30
Rook Brothers	Builders (Dodsley)	1922-38
William Etherington	Carpenter	1903-22
Edward Harper	Carpenter	1866-70
Thomas Hills	Carpenter (Lutener Rd.)	1934-38
Stephen Rook	Carpenter	1905-15
George Hoad	Coach builder	1866-74
George Dabbs	Decorator	1934-38
William Deadman	Engineer KEVII	1905-07
William Henry Oliver	Engineer KEVII	1909-24
Thomas Goldring & son	Market gardener/florist	1898-1938
Joseph Hillier	Nurseryman	1911-22
James Backshall	Wheelwright	1924-30
Edward Lickfold	Wheelwright	1845-74
Samuel Perrin	Wheelwright	1890-1909
John Dilloway	Boot maker	1845-78
John Andrews	Shoe maker	1882-1922
William Curtis	Shoe maker (Henley)	1882-87
Allan John Puttick	Shoe maker (Bexley)	1882-1903

Retailers

The advent of supermarkets has put rural shops under threat, but in this period most people bought locally. Five butchers are listed, although apart from Mark May, none stayed very long.

There were nine grocers, most of whom are described as dealers. They would have stocked many of the necessities of rural life, while Arthur Mills and son were also bakers. Six general shopkeepers are listed, including one at Bexley Hill, and five postmasters or mistresses, most of whom ran other businesses. From 1887 onwards there were also two coal merchants.

F. A. Tallant	Builders' merchant	1903-24
Arthur Henry Gillham	Butcher	1898-99
Mrs. Maria Latter	Butcher	1922-24
Mark May	Butcher	1866-95
William Smart	Butcher	1855-59
John Stubbington	Butcher	1851-52
John Burt	Coal merchant	1887-95
Arthur Gillham (Bros)	Coal merchant	1895-1938
A. J. Blaker and Son	Corn flour merchant	1883-87
James Henry Martin	Grocer	1903-09
Harry Page	Grocer	1924-38
Arthur Nelson Pearce	Grocer	1911-38
Arthur Mills & son	Grocer/Baker	1898-1909
Sarah Jane Martin	Grocer/Brewery agent	1890-99
William Damer	Grocer/dealer	1845-74
Jesse Page	Grocer/dealer	1878-99
William Page	Grocer/dealer	1898-1922
Stevens Brothers	Grocer/dealer	1898-1930
William Terry	Post office/Receiver	1855-66
Elizabeth Terry	Post office	1874-87
Eliza Baker	Post office	1887-99
Frederick Mills	Post office	1903-09
Harold F. N. Hamilton	Post office/Shopkeeper	1911-15
James William Brighty	Post office/Stationer	1918-22
William Jack Etherington	Post office/Confectioner	1924-38
George Dabbs	Shopkeeper	1855-74
Thomas Mallam	Shopkeeper	1851-52
William Martin	Shopkeeper	1855-87
Mrs. Mary Puttick	Shopkeeper (Bexley)	1870-95
Mrs. Fanny Rook	Shopkeeper (Lutener Rd.)	1909-18
Stephen Rook	Shopkeeper (Lutener Rd.)	1887-1909

There were grocers into the 1960s near the turning to Loves Farm, immediately north of the White Horse and at the east end of Lutener Road, on the south side. The shop at the south end of this block was used by Coze (see last note in this chapter), closing in the 1990s when in use for antiques. Prior to that it was a ladies hairdressers. The shop at the west end of Lutener Road (north side) closed in the 1960s, when selling hardware,

Professionals

Francis Tallant	Land agent	1870-95
Thomas Mallam	Land surveyor	1855-58
Mrs. Margaret Fuller	Nurse	1905-07
Miss E.L. Douglas	Nursing home	1930-34

Samuel Edward Stratford	Sanitary inspector (Lynton, Dodsley)	1905-38
George Herbert May	Solicitor	1913-15
Thomas Mallam	Registrar	1859-66
Edward Cooper Smith	Vet (Hollist)	1870-1913

Service providers

Charles Lane	Artist	1905-07
George Pirie	Artist	1905-07
William Oliver	Car hire/Tea rooms (Sanatorium Drive)	1934-38
Lois and Alice Harber	Dress makers (Lutener Rd.)	1905-30
Misses Harber and Puttick	Dress makers	1895-98
Henry George Pearce	Ladies hairdresser (Easebourne Lane)	1934-38
Thomas William Barnes	Motor garage (Sanatorium Drive)	1927-30
William Smith Tatner	Plumber/Gas fitter	1887-1915
Mrs. Emma Talbot	Laundress	1898-1927
Caleb Soane	Undertaker	1915-30
Francis Coze	Photographer	1898-1930

When Francis Coze opened his business in 1898 he was described as a maker of photographic equipment, but long before his last entry in 1930 he had abandoned the manufacturing side of his business. An old flyer gives his address as 11 Lutener Road.

North Mill

This was recorded in the Doomsday Book as valued at 40 shillings, presumably per annum. The next record is of a rebuilding contract in 1467. Further reconstruction took place in 1806; the miller from 1792 had been John Tipper. It was in 1826-39 William Tribe, 1851-74 John Gosden, 1874-90 John Alwyn, 1890-95 Francis Tallant, 1903-27 John Gwillam (also at Coultershaw Mill, Petworth) and 1934 onwards John Witt Mann & Son Ltd. When closed in 1966, it was in the hands of Bartholomews of Chichester. It had two low breastshot water wheels in use as late as 1957, plus a turbine which remained to the end. The premises have formed dwellings since 1970.

Source
Stidder, D & Smith, C **Watermills of Sussex** Volume II West Sussex (Published by authors).

Gillhams Garage

This developed at the east end of Lutener Road on its north side. There had been a Methodist Chapel on the adjacent site from 1882 until 1904 and Chapel Cottage was built on it in 1909. Motor Showrooms were established on the Easebourne Lane frontage and a coal merchant used the yard to the rear of it. The petrol pumps were also on the main road, but at a high level. Access was by means of six steps, which can still be seen today. The pumps were moved across the road to their present position in 1961.

Russells operated extensive motor trade premises in Midhurst, at the A286/A272 junction (now Russells Corner). The firm purchased Gillhams Garage in about 1967 and sold it to the Rootes Group in around 1970. This firm manufactured Hillman, Humber and Sunbeam Talbot cars and the showroom was used for the sale of their products. The Ford agency was thus discontinued, it going to Parkland Motors in North Street, Midhurst.

The shed adjacent to the chapel was demolished in about 1972 and its site, together with the yard between it and the showrooms, was used for the large workshop now present. The Rootes family were faced with death duty problems and sold the premises to D.B.Cragg for car body repair work. The firm went into liquidation in 1976 and the association of the buildings with the motor trade came to an end. The name of Gillham lives on as a filling station and shop on the opposite side of the road.

9.1   Gillham's Morris lorry was recorded at Heyshott in May 1942. Wartime demanded a headlamp mask (the other had no bulb) and MIDHURST to be painted over. The crew was Sidney and George Orchard. An open-top Austin was part of Gillham's taxi fleet in the 1930s; there were also two similar saloon models available.

9.2   North Mill was recorded in action on a postcard. The right part was the miller's dwelling. The finger post on the extreme right is now an exhibit at Amberley Working Museum.

9.3   On the left is Easebourne Post Office, a familiar sight in 2006. The flat roof in the distance is on part of Page's store, noted for good groceries. The business was merged with the Post Office by Mr. Jerreat in about 1970 and the projection was subsequently demolished.

9.4   Etherington's joinery workshop is centre. Coffins were also produced and funerals arranged. Easebourne Lane has a grass verge on the right and the stream in a culvert on the left. When this was piped in the 1930s during road widening an avenue of massive trees, probably elms, was lost. They stretched to North Mill.

10. Backshalls
A Family Enterprise

Easebourne has benefitted from the business activities of members of the Backshall family for nearly a century. The story is difficult to tell as there was more than one Jack Backshall and so the American system of initials and numbers will be used, although JBI and JBII were formally both John James. The present John Backshall will be similarly numbered for simplicity and continuity.

Their first premises are to be seen in the centre of picture 9.4, on the previous page.

10.1.   JBI was a wheelwright and a cartwright, these tasks requiring skills beyond most other villagers. The steel rims were heated in a large hearth and then shrunk onto the wooden wheels, with much smoke, plus steam from the cooling water.

10.2.   JBI   and   JBII   were photographed in 1913 at their premises in Easebourne Lane, opposite the churchyard west gates. Motor spirit was then the name for petrol, which was sold in two-gallon cans. "Mex" was the trade name for the products of the Mexican Oil Company in which Lord Cowdray had an interest. Backshalls later had agencies for Swift cycles and Ariel motorcycles.

10.3.   A shed was leased in Dodsley Lane in 1919. It was on the site immediately to the south of the present premises and it was used until 1927.

10.4.   Soon after the completion of the new building in 1927, a hand-cranked petrol pump was obtained. It was a Shell Mk. IV model, which had two clear glass bottles on view. One was filled while the other was drained down a rubber pipe into the car and then the cycle was repeated by the mechanic, a time consuming operation.

10.5.   An electric pump was acquired in 1945 and these pumps followed in 1953, along with council houses nearby. JBII had died in 1929 leaving JBI to run the business with the help of young JBIII, who had an engineering training and joined the firm in 1923. JBI died following a road accident in 1937, leaving JBIII to develop the business, but enforced closure took place in May 1940, following the advent of World War II. The workshop was used for military battery production during the war. The sign refers to M. Backshall. This was Minnie, but she was too young to run a business in the eyes of the law. Minnie was the aunt of JBIII.

10.6.   A new building, with a flat on the first floor, was erected in 1956 and is seen in 1982, along with the 1976 workshop behind. On the right is JBIV with one of the firm's hire vehicles. They had a hire fleet from 1979 to 1985. The workshop and the northern part of the frontage was leased to the Rotherfield Motor Company from 1st April 1988, but John Backshall (JBIV) continued to serve the community with fuel and a well stocked shop until his retirement on 31st March 2005. The commendable service to the parish had been established by his great grandfather 94 years earlier. The retail business was leased to K&I Garages of Pulborough.

✎ 11. Communications ✎

Origins of the Telephones

The Midhurst telephone exchange and call office opened on 4th August 1909. It was connected by a trunk line to Petersfield in the Southampton zone. Originally it had 21 subscribers, one of whom, Thomas Goldring and son, florists of West Street, Midhurst, had a market garden in Dodsley.

The charges for a three minute call (day rate) were 6d to London and 4s 6d to Glasgow. Since many people were only earning £1 or £2 per week, these fees were very high and probably discouraged the initial growth of the network, or even the use of the telephone except in emergency.

Originally the hours of attendance were 4.30 a.m. to 10.15 p.m. on weekdays and 4.30 a.m. to 10 a.m. and 7.30 p.m. to 9.45 p.m. on Sundays. Advertisements in the first directory claimed "A Telephone in the house lessens the labour of housekeeping and brings the tradesman to your door.' There was also a message for non-subscribers, 'The Public Telephone Call Rooms place the vast facilities of the telephone system at the disposal of everyone.'

By January 1910 public call offices had been opened at Easebourne Post Office and King Edward VII Sanatorium and 18 months later there were 35 subscribers with three in Easebourne.

Lord Cowdray and the Estate Office were on line by January 1912 together with the Guardians of the Workhouse. In April 1911, the latter had received a quotation from the Superintendent Engineer Post Office Telegraphs Department for connecting the Workhouse to the Midhurst Rural District Council office by telephone, and the office to the trunk on a three-year contract.

They also enquired about an additional line from the office to a fireman's home. (The risk of fire was appreciable, 11 years earlier the Westhampnett Workhouse had burnt down). However this extension would cost £1/12/- so they settled instead for an extension bell at 5/-. They also decided on separate lines to the workhouse and to the office, and each evening before the exchange closed down, the two were connected at the cost of one exchange call per night.

By July 1912 the number of Midhurst subscribers had risen to 41 although there were no more in Easebourne. In October 1916 the service became continuous, and the Workhouse Guardians were saved the cost of 365 calls per year. However a few months later, they received an all too familiar letter from the Post Office, the rates were going up!

After the war Midhurst became part of the Guildford zone. In September 1922, the exchange had 74 lines and 115 stations (this latter number includes extensions), while ten years later the corresponding figures were 235 and 330.

A directory issued in September 1920 listed seven private subscribers in Easebourne and seven business users. In September 1922 there were four more business users and in March 1923 three more private ones.

Another indication of the growth of the commercial section comes from the Kelly's Directories. In 1911 it only listed two Easebourne lines at King Edward VII Hospital and the Workhouse, and there was just one new entry in 1913.

In 1927, 19 users are listed for the first time, with three more in 1930, two in 1934 and 11 in 1938. The businesses included public houses, tea gardens, a nursing home, a decorator, farmers and farm bailiffs, an undertaker, a sanitary inspector, the Cottage Hospital and a petrol filling station.

First occurrence of telephone listing in directory or Kelly's

Private subscribers	First listing
Baker-Carr Major H (Buddington Farm)	Sept 1920
Betts Rev H.P. (Buddington House)	March 1923
Bourdillon F.W. (Buddington)	July 1911
Combe Nigel V J.P.(Hollist)	Sept 1920
Cowdray Lord	Jan 1912
Cozens-Brooke Percy (Buddington Farm)	Sept 1922
Faskin Major General C. (Highlands Easebourne)	March 1923
Fitzwilliam G.J.C.W. (Old Vicarage Easebourne)	March 1923
Harding-Newman Major F.R. (Rotherfield House)	Sept 1922
Koch W.O. (Easebourne Lane).	July 1911
Johnston W (Bybrook, Easebourne)	Sept 1922
Johnstone W (Park Cottage)	Sept 1920
Pearson Major The Hon H (Rotherfield House)	Sept 1920
Sharrock C. W. (Easebourne)	Sept 1920

Trade subscribers	First listing
Aburrow Frank Beresford (Farmer)	Kelly 1938
Backshall M & J (Filling station)	Kelly 1938
Bridger Richard (Farmer)	Kelly 1938
Brighty J.W. (Stationer, newsagent, tobacco, PO)	Sept 1922
Brown Mrs. W. M. (Tea garden)	Kelly 1927
Cooper Frederick John (Farmer)	Kelly 1927
Cowdray Estate Office	July 1911
Crescent Lodge (Nursing home)	Kelly 1930
Dabbs George (Decorator)	Kelly 1938
Easebourne Village Institute	Kelly 1927
Edwards Frederick J (Gardener, Lord Cowdray)	Kelly 1927
Etherington (Builders)	Kelly 1927
Gillham A. (Coal oil merchants)	Sept 1920
Gingell Frederick (Farm bailiff)	Kelly 1927
Goldring Thomas & son (Market gardeners, Florist)	Kelly 1927
Gwillim J (Miller, North Mill)	July 1911
Haber Lois & Alice (Dressmakers)	Kelly 1927
King Edward VII Sanatorium (Second line)	Kelly 1938
Langdale Arthur Marmaduke (Farm bailiff)	Kelly 1938
Marris Owen F (Grocer)	Kelly 1934
Midhurst and Easebourne Cottage Hospital	Kelly 1930
Midhurst Union Workhouse	Jan 1912
Moseley John (Holly Tree)	Kelly 1927
Oliver William (Car hire, tea rooms)	Kelly 1934
Page Harry (Grocer)	Kelly 1938
Parham Charles E.H. (assistant overseer PC clerk)	Kelly 1927
Partridge Oliver (White Horse)	Kelly 1927
Pearce Arthur Nelson (Grocer)	Kelly 1938
Pearce Henry George (Ladies hairdresser)	Kelly 1938
Pollard William J (Duke of Cumberland)	Kelly 1927

Trade subscriber (continued)

Rook Brothers (Builders)	Kelly 1938
Soane Caleb (Undertaker)	Kelly 1930
Stevens Bros. (Grocers, wine, hardware)	Sept 1920
Stratford Samuel Edward (Sanitary inspector)	Kelly 1927
Talbot Mrs. Emma (Laundress)	Kelly 1927
Walder Charles (Rother Inn)	Kelly 1927

Sources
Cole, M. (B.T. Achives).

Post Office

The first reference to the Royal Mail likely to have affected Easebourne concerned a robbery in 1798 at North Heath when the horse post James Dudman was stopped by two men and the bags from Arundel, Petworth and Midhurst were taken. The perpetrators were William and Robert Drewitt who were convicted at Sussex Lent Assizes in 1799 and hung in chains at North Heath near Eastbourne (sic). From this it is clear that although the Royal Mail started using coaches in 1784 by 1798 they were still using a horse post on the then route from Arundel to Petworth and to Haslemere via Midhurst and records indicate that it is very unlikely that Royal Mail Coaches ever called at Easebourne.

However, sub-post office records dating from the mid-nineteenth century show that on 29 July 1848 Easebourne was issued with an undated circular handstamp under Petworth, an indication that a Receiving House/sub-post office was already open or was opened at that date and is the first reference in GPO records. There are also other mentions from that time gleaned from post office archives and directories. They are not complete and do not state where the Receiving House or Sub-Post Office was, although the position usually moved around with the holder of the office so that if any of the names mentioned was the licensee of the White Horse, then that is a strong indication that the White Horse was also the Receiving House.

1855/9	The Receiver was Anthony Terry with mail received from Petworth.
1859	Easebourne was transferred under Midhurst
1886	Easebourne was issued with a rubber handstamp
1890	Easebourne became a Money Order and Savings Bank office.
1908	Easebourne became a telegraph office with code ESB
1913/5	Harold Hamilton was the shopkeeper and sub-postmaster
1922	James Brighty was the sub-postmaster as well as a school attendance officer
1946	Easebourne became a rural town sub office

Midhurst Television Mast

In the 1960s the Midhurst area received television on the 405-line system from Crystal Palace in London and Rowridge on the Isle of Wight. But with the advent of the 625-line format, broadcast at a higher frequency, many more transmitters were necessary.

There was urgent need for a substation to serve West Sussex, but it was difficult to find a suitable location for the tall mast required, since there were four airfields in the vicinity at Tangmere, Dunsfold, Goodwood and Gatwick. The one practical site was a small area of Bexley Hill in Easebourne.

The BBC made preliminary tests using signals transmitted from a barrage balloon tethered above the hill, and in February 1968 approached the Planning and Rights of Way Committee of Midhurst Rural District Council. They applied for outline planning permission and by November had had discussions with the Sussex Rural Community Council about the environmental impact.

In January 1969 two BBC representatives explained the technical aspects of the project. They considered that a 350-foot tower at an altitude of 500 feet would provide an excellent service for the neighbourhood together with a relay station at Haslemere. Services would include BBC colour and commercial channels and the system could be extended later. The transmitter building and 11,000-volt supply line would be hidden by trees, and they had obtained the permission of the landowners, the Cowdray Estate. However if the plan were rejected, it would be necessary to build three or more smaller masts to serve the area.

In order to assess the visual impact the BBC offered to fly a balloon at the proposed height of the mast. The first test in February 1969 ended prematurely when the cord broke and the balloon disappeared and it was six months before this could be repeated. Inevitably there were objections from individuals and amenity groups but in September the BBC unveiled plans to raise the height of the mast from 350 to 550 feet to improve coverage.

West Sussex County Council approved this new application, but following discussions with the Board of Trade and users of light aircraft the proposed height of the mast was reduced to 375 feet and fresh planning permission was required.

The final site chosen was north of Grevetts Common and west of Bexley Hill Common three miles northeast of Midhurst. In May 1971 the BBC placed a contract with Messrs Chapman, Lowry and Puttick of Haslemere to construct the transmission building and British Insulated Callender Construction Ltd of Thornton Heath to design and erect the mast. This was completed by the end of the year apart from the installation of the aerial. Fortunately the mast was less obtrusive than expected and the visual impact considerably less than for the power pylons crossing the hill.

It was hoped to start transmissions the next summer, but the system was still being tested in late autumn. BBC 1 and 2 began transmissions on 4th December 1972 with the commercial channel, then franchised to Southern Television, a fortnight later covering an area from Burgess Hill to Bordon and from Ockley to the Downs.

Thirteen airline companies began using the mast as a navigation aid, although allegedly the light on top was switched on each night by a man travelling by bicycle! The station was sabotaged in the early hours of Friday, 9th February 1979, by men using sledgehammers who entered the unmanned building and did damage estimated at £17,000 to the BBC transmitters and cutting service to 100,000 homes. Although temporary repairs were made in a few hours, it took a week to return to normal.

The station transmitted analogue signals, but in 2000 these were augmented by a digital system. With just six separate signals, it was possible to broadcast 30 or more channels simultaneously and it was decided to shut down the analogue service completely by 2012.

In December 2003, Midhurst became the 18th station to be added to the DAB digital radio network. Apart from a considerable improvement in sound quality, it gave local listeners access to programmes such as Radio 1 to 7, Five Live Sports Extra, the World Service and various commercial channels.

Bus Services

These notes refer to weekday services.

The first record found of a bus through the village was on 27th April 1913, when Haslemere Car Hirers began a service. It was taken over by Aldershot & District Traction Co. Ltd on 15th November of that year as no. 19. It was discontinued for part of the war, but in August 1919 a minute stated that the "Midhurst service has been reopened".

The route 19 was extended to Chichester in June 1921. It was further extended to Bognor Regis in 1924. The section of the route through Easebourne had a 30-minute interval from July 1928. World War II made Midhurst the southern terminus of the route until 1946.

The company operated a trip between Haslemere station and the King Edward VII Sanatorium on Sundays from August 1934; it was numbered 19A.

Southdown Motor Services started service 40 between Horsham and Chichester via Easebourne on 1st April 1924. From this date some buses from Aldershot continued to Bognor Regis. No. 40 became 60 in 1927 and then 59 in 1935. Route 61 from Horsham to Petersfield started in September 1947. Nos 59 and 61 both ceased on 11th June 1955, being replaced by the no. 22 from Brighton. It ran through to Petersfield for three years. Subsequently, buses from Petersfield used Lutener Road for turning, until the bus stands were built in Midhurst in about 1964.

Aldershot buses ran every half-hour to Midhurst station until it closed in 1955. Subsequently, they turned by reversing into Grange Road. One every two hours continued to Bognor until 1969. They became hourly in September 1963 and were numbered 219 from September 1974 after A&D merged with Thames Valley in 1972.

Southdown route 22 operated between Brighton and Midhurst until May 1968, serving the village hourly. Thereafter, the buses from Petersfield on routes 59 and 61 were extended to Petworth, still offering an hourly service. A year later, these routes were extended to Brighton, still hourly. One trip was cut back to Pulborough in November 1971 and the interval was increased to two hours, the other journeys being between Worthing and Midhurst. These were numbered 201 and ran until May 1980. Thereafter, there were only two such workings, plus five from Petworth, but these ceased in 1986.

From October 1986, Alder Valley ran four trips to Petworth and three to Pulborough, using the number 225. From that time, there has been a useful Saturday afternoon return journey between Petworth and Portsmouth, this still operating 20 years later.

Short periods of irregular operation were provided by Sussex Bus and Cedar Travel. The latter used minibuses from September 1990 and ran two trips to Petworth and four to Storrington, on behalf of Sussex Bus, using the number c20. This service ceased in October 1991 and Alder Valley 225 returned until May 1993, when Stagecoach route no. 1 took over, operating to Worthing hourly. This still applied in 2006.

Richardson Travel, trading as AST (Travel), began a Midhurst Town Service on 4th January 1993. It ran on a figure of 8 route, Easebourne being the top part and Holmbush the lower. Thus the village had three operators providing the best service ever. Competition came in 1994 with the advent of the Midhurst Community Bus. Stagecoach took over the figure of 8 in 1997 as route 99 and banned passengers from using more than half of it. Thus they were forced to wait uncomfortably in the town and the service was withdrawn in 2001. It was replaced by extending some 91 and 92 buses from Petersfield to King Edward VII, via the village centre. These continued despite closure of the hospital in March 2006.

Services to Lodsworth, Lurgashall and Northchapel are not described, as they ran infrequently on different days of the week. They were operated by Hants & Sussex, Southern Motorways, Sussex Bus and Stagecoach over a period of about 75 years, but disappeared at the start of the 21st century. However, DORiS came to the rescue of those needing transport away from existing bus services. The bus began operation in July 2000.

The Aldershot service was cut back to Haslemere in 1987 and numbered 229. It lasted ten years, after which Stagecoach no. 60 operated hourly between Bognor Regis and Guildford. A further two years and it became no. 70 and terminated at Midhurst, with an unhelpful one and a half hour gap at both peak periods.

For simplicity these notes exclude school and Sunday services, also the Brighton-Salisbury Tuesday buses of the 1990s, which did not stop in the village.

Sources
Public timetables
Allpress J. (Southdown) unpublished
Lambert A. (Southdown) unpublished
Trevaskis P. (A&D) unpublished

11.1   No photograph of an A & D in the village is available and so this Dennis is shown outside the Grammar School on 6th February 1956, next stop Easebourne. Included are the petrol pumps of Midhurst Engineering and the conical tower of the Town Hall. (P. Trevaskis)

11.2   Northbound in Easebourne Lane on 29th September 1995 is the Mercedes of AST on the circular service, which ran mostly at 30-minute intervals. The lamp was once on Selham station.

11.3   One mile of the railway between Midhurst and Pulborough passed through Easebourne parish, west of Ambersham Common. Regular passenger trains ceased on 5th February 1955 and goods on 16th October 1964. This is the penultimate railtour, approaching Midhurst Tunnel on 23rd June 1962. The bridge is in West Lavington and is still in use.

11.4   While bus service improved, telephone did not. Wheelbarrow Castle lost its kiosk in 2005.

11.5   Road communication on the A272 ceased for ten days from 2nd May 1992, following the spillage of tons of slippery oil-well drilling slurry; for some hours the smelly compound was a mystery to all concerned. Eventually a dam was built across the road to prevent watercourse pollution, but the clean-up proved very difficult; the prosecution was unsuccessful, despite the obvious facts.

11.6   Despite closure of the hospital, buses continued to run to its site and to provide Easebourne with an enhanced service. The rustic elm shelter (right) arrived in 1967 and the urban one opposite came pre-vandalised from Crawley, shortly before this view of a Sussex Bus was taken on 26th May 2003.

12. Leisure

Polo

Yolanda Carslaw

One of the oldest known games, its origins can be traced back to Manipur state, India, about 300BC. It is also claimed to be of Persian origin as a game known as "Pulu" about 525BC. First played in England in 1869 it was brought to Cowdray Park by Harold Pearson, late 2nd Viscount Cowdray in 1910.

Midhurst's polo club, Cowdray Park, is the sport's European epicentre. Every summer, players from all over the world converge here for the Cowdray Park Gold Cup, the most important tournament this side of the Atlantic. The game has a strong local following, but on Gold Cup final day a crowd of 15,000 assembles at the Lawns, beyond Cowdray Ruins, to watch the showdown.

Polo is thought to be the oldest team game in the world. The first recorded match was in Iran around 600 BC but the game was also played in the far east in antiquity. It came to the west via the Indian state of Manipur through the enthusiasm of the British Cavalry and the first game in England was played in 1869 between the 9th and 10th Lancers.

Spread by the military, the game gathered pace in Britain and its colonies; clubs were set up nationwide and worldwide and rules were drawn up. The pitch is 300 yards long and about 150 wide, and two teams of four play a series of seven-minute 'chukkas' with a change of pony between each.

Harold Pearson, later the second Viscount Cowdray, played polo at Oxford, captaining the side in 1905. He brought the game to Cowdray in 1910, laying out the House Ground – in front of Cowdray House – and later the Lawns and River Grounds – near Cowdray Ruins, almost within sight of Midhurst. Early fixtures included Goodwood Week, with teams like Harold's Capron House competing for the Cowdray Park Challenge Cup – a prize still played for today. Polo was a social as well as sporting occasion, with villagers encouraged to watch and given refreshments.

Between the wars the game enjoyed a 'golden age', especially at England's principal clubs in London. At Cowdray in 1926, 3000 spectators watched the Challenge Cup. In 1927, the first Viscount Cowdray died, then his son, Harold, died in 1933 aged only 51. The 23-year-old third Viscount, John, took over. Though the club continued to prosper, the Second World War had a devastating effect on the game, with London's most important clubs and grounds closed down, never to reopen. At the same time, with mechanisation in the military, the supply of cavalry officers – a vital source of players – dried up.

John Cowdray revived play in 1947, but as ponies and players were short, sides were reduced to three and ladies were included. He joined in despite having lost his left arm at Dunkirk – he held the reins with a hook. During Goodwood Week in 1948, seven teams competed and he received an invitation to play in Argentina, an event which boosted the English game. Thanks to his dedication, Cowdray Park quickly became polo's chief venue, and the Coronation cup of 1953 attracted 15,000 spectators including the Queen and Prince Philip, who became a good player himself, winning the Gold Cup twice in the 1960s. In 1956, the first Gold Cup took place.

Following Cowdray's lead, other clubs – new and old – found their feet and polo recovered nationwide. By the 1980s it had shifted from an amateur game to one dominated by professionals paid by playing 'patrons'. The best professionals came from Argentina, which also supplied the choice ponies, but the Falklands War of 1982 temporarily interrupted this source. The 1990s were marked by the arrival at Stedham of Kerry Packer, who laid grounds of such quality that Cowdray Park decided to improve its own, putting in new grounds at the Lawns and relaying its existing Lawns ground.

John Cowdray died in 1995 and the fourth Viscount, Michael Pearson, took over. Unlike his younger brother, he does not play, but the club continues to thrive. In 2006, it had 150 playing members and 850 social members, and its grounds are regarded as the best in Britain. It has ten of its own – five at Ambersham and five at the Lawns and River (the House Ground is no longer used by the club), and also uses Brooksfield, a ground next to Ambersham laid by patron Brook Johnson, and the three grounds at Stedham laid by Kerry Packer. In addition, the club generates a massive seasonal industry as teams, players and their entourages descend on the Midhurst district from April to September.

Cowdray's chairman until 2002 was Charles Fraser, who is married to John Cowdray's daughter, Lucy. Since then, the chairman has been David Jamison, a Graffham-based former patron who has lifted the Gold Cup four times.

Sources:
"Polo at Cowdray" published 1992. Derek Russell-Stoneham and Roger Chatterton-Newman.

Golf Club

The Cowdray Course may well have started with an odd number of holes laid out for the enjoyment of Lord Egmont, as this is how the game evolved, and an anecdote recorded in **Southern Golf**, of May 1981, mentions Charles Bowyer (owner of Chemist shops in Midhurst and Petworth) as having visited the course in 1900. However, the first record, a scorecard printed in 1907, clearly shows a full 18 hole layout and appears to be set out for use by the public at large and relates to both medal and matchplay. Notes made by the Second Viscount Cowdray refer to the course as it existed in 1909 after purchase from Lord Egmont and indicate that it was laid out some years earlier by Jack White, for over 20 years professional at Sunningdale, where he won the British Open Championship in 1904. It is not until 1920 that there is mention of players forming a club but, unlike the majority of clubs at that time, it has never had an artisans' section and has always been a fully integrated social grouping representative of the local community.

Regulation 7 on the scorecard referring to notices in the golf hut give us the clue that the first location of a members' facility would most probably have been the old cricket pavilion sited next to the cricket ground and where Canadian troops were camped during the Second World War. Few records exist from this period but, with the formation of the members' club, the need for a clubhouse emerged. On 16th June 1954 Weetman John Churchill Pearson, Third Viscount Cowdray, opened the first real clubhouse, a post war concrete tile hung building.

The patronage of the Pearson family has had a huge influence on the development of golf at Cowdray but by the 1990s the Cowdray family were no longer active participants in the game and the course needed investment and 'in house' facilities were well below standard. Therefore a recovery plan was put into operation which included major course improvements. An entirely new clubhouse was opened by The Fourth Viscount Cowdray in 2002 and the old clubhouse was converted into a golf lodge with 8 bedrooms, the work being carried out by Cowdray Park craftsmen, all this adding a new dimension to this prestigious Club.

Sources:
"100 years of Golf at Cowdray Park", published in 2004.

Stoolball

Stoolball in various guises has been played for at least 600 or 700 years and may be the ancestor of cricket, rounders and baseball. Initially it involved one person throwing a ball at the base of a milkmaid's stool, which another attempted to defend with their hand or a bat. Later the stool was replaced by a square target on a post, and a scoring system like cricket was introduced; with the batsman hitting the ball and running to another wicket 16 yards away from where the ball had been bowled. The playing area is a circle 90 yards in diameter and most players are women, in teams of eleven (or eight in tournaments) although some men do also compete.

Rules were drawn up in 1881, and the game was popularised during the First World War by a Major W.W.Grantham to provide some sport for the "battered heroes of the war in our military hospitals". It is still widely played in Sussex and the adjoining parts of Kent, Surrey and Hampshire and being quite competitive is not recommended for faint hearted umpires!"

Local interest goes back at least 90 years, Easebourne and Midhurst field teams and in summer both the Rotherfield and Cowdray grounds are used with an indoor version taking place at the Grange Centre in Midhurst.

Sources
"Stoolball is alive and well in Sussex" Martin Hoerchner 2002, SABR UK Website.

Midhurst & Easebourne Cricket Clubs

The year 1806 is generally accepted for the formation of the Midhurst Cricket Club, but it has recently been discovered that there is a record of a match between Midhurst and Easebourne on the 12th July 1754. "The odds on Midhurst side was 6 to 5 before they began to play, but Easebourne beat them by 43 notches at first innings, so that many who backed Midhurst was taken in". It is also recorded that in 1802 in Esburn (Easebourne Park) John Howard of Storrington scored 110 not out for North Sussex v. South Sussex, the first Sussex century. Perhaps it can be said that the Midhurst Cricket Club actually started in Easebourne! There are records that the club played at Bepton and in 1914 the ground was used as a prisoner of war camp. Cricket was resumed in 1920 and the club moved to the present grounds situated at Cowdray Ruins. Although it is known as the Midhurst Cricket Club, its roots definitely started in Easebourne and games are also played on Rotherfield.

Midhurst and Easebourne United Football Club

Like any football club it has had ups and downs but it is still thriving. Have a look at their Football Club History database; to mention a few highlights - '81-'82 season, promoted to division one, later relegated to division two then division three. In 1999 they left Sussex County League only to rejoin in the 2002-3 season and promoted to division two! Why not watch a game or two at their home grounds off Dodsley Lane on a Saturday? The Midhurst Rugby Club also plays in Easebourne, on the ground near The Ruins.

Rother Angling Club

The Rother Angling Club was formed in 1952 and based at the White Horse Inn at Easebourne. The only water at the time was the River Rother at North Mill, and membership was 7/6d per year, or 2/6d for a day ticket. Few documented records survive from the early years and Committee meetings seem to have been held on an "as and when" basis. However, a thriving angling club soon developed and by 1962 money was being spent on fish. When they arrived, the river was in flood so members dammed a stream in a field opposite the Holly Tree pub and the fish spent just over a week in there until the river level had returned to normal.

In 1969 the Club took on a rather muddy puddle, and with a lot of work it was turned into what we now know as Rotherfield Pond. It was the members who dug this out by hand and with various pieces of improvised machinery. The Club secured another stretch of river upstream of North Mill at Woolbeding in 1971.

In 1978 New Pond was added to the ever-increasing list of Club venues and Mr Sainsbury arrived at Woolbeding. He objected to seeing anglers fishing opposite his house so the National Trust requested a move to the stretch upstream of the bridge. At least this gave a longer stretch of water.

Rother Angling Club first entered a team in the Central Southern Junior Angling League in 1979 and this set the scene for many such successful competitive future events.

Sources
Wagham, DC. 29 Squires P.V.S.C. 11.
The Rother Angling Club, "The First 50 years", produced in 2002.

Easebourne Allotments

It is said that these allotments, like many others in the country, were started in the early days of the Second World War, but they were common in the 19th century. Some were shown on the 1897 map in Canada Grove and Glaziers Lane. They are still thriving well and the Easebourne Garden & Allotment Society hold regular meetings and enjoy outings. During the war years (and no doubt for a long time afterwards), allotments produced more than 10% of the national vegetable produce!

Public Houses

The landlords' initial year of tenancy is shown in brackets, but there may be some minor errors as the directories were only published every three or four years. The records shown below are otherwise complete up to 1939. The dates refer to entries in Kelly's Directory.

White Horse. John Ayling 1839, George Luff 1845, William Chitty 1850, Henry Horn 1855, John Boxall 1858, James Woolgar 1862, James Shepperd 1866, George Stewart 1874, George Saunders 1882, Mrs Mary Ann Saunders 1898, George Harrison 1903, George Harrison and Oliver Partridge 1918.

Rother Inn. Arthur Mills 1882, Frederick Webster 1903, Mrs Frederick Webster 1909, Edward Robert Latter 1911, Mrs Maria Rawlingson 1922, Charles Henry Walder 1927, Harry F. Wheatland 1938. It was situated on the south side of Lutener Road and was part of the major building work of the early 1880s. It is marked as P.H. on map IV and was in use until 1994, the last licensee being Phil James.

Duke of Cumberland. James West 1882, Joseph Moseley 1890, Thomas Puttick 1895, Daniel Vennes 1898, Thomas Wood 1915, William J. Pollard 1927.

The Holly Tree. John Moseley 1927 probably upon opening, but no other details available. It closed in September 2004 and was in Easebourne Street, north of the junction with Wick Lane.

The Plough & Harrow. Its location is shown on map I. The building was erected in 1707 and it became a public house from a later date until 1804. The 1847 map shows it as an inn again, but later it was also listed as a smithy.

Youth Organisations

It is very much regretted that from the records available it has not been possible to compile an accurate or full list of the leaders of the Scouting and Guiding Units. Apologies are sincerely offered for this omission, also to any whose achievements have been left out for the same reason.

Scouts - It is thought that the group, which is still officially named "1st Easebourne Lady Cowdray's Own", started with the Scouts around 1912, with an unbroken record to the present day. Cubs followed on, continuing until 1973, restarting in 1986 and ongoing. Rovers opened in 1927 but were disbanded in 1939. With the advent of Venture Scouts and Beavers, a Venture Scout Group started in 1992, closing in 1994, reopening in 2000 and continuing, as are Beavers which were started in 1993.

In the early years the units met in various local buildings including The Refectory, The Barn (off Wheelbarrow Castle, now Highfield Close), in the Institute and, from 1956, in the Hut next to the Institute. However, with units growing in numbers, a new HQ was built in the wood east of the Church and opened by Robert Windle (Cowdray Estate Manager) in 1992.

To emphasise the worldwide family of Scouting, the Venture Scouts went to Belgium and France on "European Venture", meeting up with thousands of brother Scouts and in 1995 members of the unit joined with neighbouring Sussex units to attend a week's camp in Southern Holland with a day trip to the World Jamboree. In 1999 they visited Finland.

Proud moments for the Scouts came in 2002 when, under the leadership of Chris Davis, five Venture Scouts were presented with their Queens Scout Award at Windsor Castle and in 2006, when five Cubs completed a series of challenges to earn the Chief Scout's Silver Award, the highest award available to Cubs.

Guides - Guiding has thrived in Easebourne since January 22nd 1919 when the 1st Easebourne Company of the Girl Guides was registered. The only break in its long history being from 1946, when it was disbanded until 1966. At this time, it was re-registered under the leadership of Mrs Joy Mitchell. Former Queens Guide, Mrs Philippa Denman (née Mitchell), took over from her mother as Captain of the Company in 1989 and in 2006, under her leadership, Emma Parry earned her Baden-Powell Award, the highest accolade in Guiding.

Brownies - There are no written records of the early days of the Easebourne Brownie Pack, but it is known that Brownies were introduced into the village by 1927 and thought that Miss Doreen Buss was the first leader. However a Pack was not officially registered until 1966 when Mrs Barbara Mitchell opened the 1st Easebourne Brownies which met in Conifers School. An overspill of members in 1973, prompted the need for a 2nd Easebourne Unit. Mrs Mitchell started this while Mrs Louis Cooper took over the 1st Easebourne Pack, but in 2001 the two Units were amalgamated and the 1st Easebourne Brownie Pack, eighty years on, continues to flourish under the leadership of Mrs Julie Wain.

Rainbows - Mrs Alison Davis founded the Easebourne unit in 1990, soon after the inauguration of Rainbows into the Guide Movement and she continues to provide an exciting welcome to little girls, aged 5-7 years, starting out in this worldwide organisation.

Sources - Ron and Daphne Wakeford, Alison Davis, Paula Morrison, Joy Mitchell

12.1   The 1st Easebourne Guide Company was not expected to smile when photographed on 8th May 1921 at the Midhurst & District Guides' Rally.

12.2   Cricket has been played close to The Ruins for generations. This Christmas card is about a century old and is annotated MIDHURST GRAMMAR SCHOOL CRICKET GROUND.

12.3 The Easebourne Institute occupied the former Catholic Church buildings, which are centre and left. The boiler shed was an unfortunate addition aesthetically. Three of the Catholic Priests are buried in the churchyard of St. Mary's.

12.4 The opening of the new Scout Hut near the Institute was recorded in 1956.

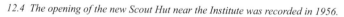

13. Cottage Hospital

Origins

The Midhurst, Easebourne and District Cottage Hospital, now known as The Midhurst Community Hospital has served the district for 80 years. However our knowledge of its history is fragmentary; few records were kept in the early days, and most of the later archives were destroyed when the building underwent major modification in the year 2000.

Writing in the Parish Magazine in July 1974, Miss Barbara Gayford, described how it was the "beloved brain child" of Dr. Bernard Bailey, a "tremendous character" who founded it around 1926. One keen supporter was Mr Bill Bevan, headmaster of Easebourne School from 1927 to 1960. The Hospital was supported by voluntary contributions, and money was raised by "Dr Bailey's Fête", held annually in his garden.

The first building was on the corner of Egmont Road and Easebourne Lane. Built in the early 20th century as a private house, Beryl. Lady Cowdray took it over as accommodation for district nurses, before passing it to the Hospital.

Miss Gayford who later founded Conifers school in the same building, wrote 'how well I remember the colour scheme - dark chocolate paint everywhere, with violent electric blue or mustard yellow on the walls. The house was heated entirely by open fires, with an antiquated kitchener for cooking. Imagine running a hospital under these conditions! Gas was not even laid on, nor were there any electric power points. There was a row of young fir trees closely packed along the northern side, making the rooms depressingly dark.'

Despite this the Hospital was an immediate success and was usually full. But although Dr. Bailey was fond of the building he thought it very inconvenient, and early in 1928 announced plans to build an annexe. An appeal raised over £1500 in less than six weeks

A new site?

In May 1929 Miss Florence Wilson suggested that the Hospital should move to Rotherfield House off Dodsley Lane. This was also owned by Lord Cowdray and had been occupied by Major Harding-Newman, his agent.

Described as a substantial modern residence built of stone, it had three reception rooms, a billiard room and 11 bedrooms, with some centrally heated and lit by electric light. There was a servants hall, kitchen, scullery, walled kitchen garden with three greenhouses, two cottages, stabling for four horses and accommodation for cows, pigs and poultry. The 19-acre estate even included a cricket ground.

Lord Cowdray dismissed her idea since he thought the running costs would be prohibitive; it was larger than required and he preferred the idea of building an annexe in Egmont Road. But then at a public meeting two months later, he claimed that the Committee were "on the wrong track", and that the money should be used to build the front of a new hospital. He had contributed £1000 to the funds through the books of the Cowdray Golf Links, and was prepared to double his donation and provide them with a site.

Move to Rotherfield House

However the option of Rotherfield House remained open. In April 1931, Lord Cowdray wrote to Mrs Harding Newman, honorary secretary of the Cottage Hospital explaining why he did not wish to rent them the property. However if the Committee were serious about moving, he was prepared to sell it to them at a low price with the option of repurchasing it at the same figure. He would retain the cricket ground and stable buildings but would let them have the rest at £3000, half its market value.

The Hospital transferred there, probably in 1932. On 8th November that year, its status was clarified when a Declaration of Trust was signed between Viscount Cowdray, Bernard Bailey, William Johnston and Harold Stone of Barclays Bank, all of whom were named as trustees. It would be an unincorporated charitable institution, known as Midhurst and District Cottage Hospital "founded for the reception, relief and cure of sick persons from time to time afflicted by accident or disease". It had no endowment and was wholly supported by voluntary contributions, with the control of the funds and management being in the hands of a committee.

Lord Cowdray died in 1933 and a plaque records that 'Beryl Viscountess Cowdray presented this house and grounds as a memorial to her husband Weetman Harold Miller 2nd Viscount Cowdray November 1934.' A formal Deed of Gift was signed on 25th October 1935 in which it was stated that the building was 'now occupied and used as a cottage hospital.' Following the gift, a new ward was built, known as the Bailey Unit, and an operating theatre was added together with outpatient and X ray facilities.

Admissions Register

Some idea of the activity of the hospital can be gained from a surviving admissions register. In a ten-month period in 1935/6 there were 169 admissions, 41% of which came from Midhurst and Easebourne, and others from as far away as Chichester, Tillington and Liphook. Almost 60% were discharged within a fortnight, although one patient stayed for 29 weeks and there were five deaths.

Much of the work involved children, half the patients were aged 24 or less, although there was one individual of 91. There were also 87 operations, over half of which were minor, the removal of tonsils, adenoids and dentistry, but some were more serious, such as the removal of kidney stones, excision of a cancerous bowel and amputation of a woman's breast. They also handled emergencies, such as bicycle and motorbike accidents and a man who had severed the tendons of his wrist.

Funding

Most of the running costs of the Hospital were met by a group of subscribers, but patients were also charged. The admissions register gives details of 134 individuals; 82 (61%) presented a card, (presumably a health care scheme), another 39 (29%) paid a fee and 13 (10%) were treated free.

In 1948 the Hospital became part of the National Health Service under the Chichester and Graylingwell Hospital Management Committee. In March 1956 the League of Friends of the Hospital was founded, providing much needed extra equipment and amenities for the patients.

Inventory and Requisition Book

An idea of the hospital layout can be gained from rooms listed in an inventory of December 1952. The Night Sister and Night Probationer had bedrooms on the top floor, and there were five bedrooms for nurses and a staff bathroom on the first. The Matron had a bedroom, sitting room and office, and the Sister a bed sitting room.

There were three single rooms for private patients with adjacent bathroom and one for emergencies. The male and female wards had four and eight beds respectively. The operating theatre was provided with sterilising and anaesthetic rooms and a darkroom for X ray films. Other facilities included a linen cupboard, later transformed into the main office and by 1956 a reading room.

A memorandum book covering the years 1967-9 lists various requisitions for equipment and supplies but there are also receipts for garden produce. The Hospital was not only producing its own vegetables, but also sold some to other institutions such as Graylingwell.

1967-8

Fortuitously many official records have been preserved for the period June 1967 to December 1968. Typical among these is a summary, comparing the performance of the Hospital in the first half of 1968 with that of 1967.

Numbers are fairly similar between the two periods. About two operations a month were performed, but there was an increase in the average duration of stay from 28.6 to 41.6 days and an increase in the number of pathology samples taken. Outpatients were seen on average two or three times each.

Staffing was a chronic problem throughout this period and the Hospital had a "hand to mouth existence." It was very difficult to recruit nursing auxiliaries since this was a time of financial constraint, and cadets from the British Red Cross often helped on Saturday mornings. Most patients were elderly and required extra care, in December 1968, 15 out of 16 were aged 80 or above.

Many general practitioners were unwilling to admit patients in view of the scarcity of nurses particularly in the evenings and at weekends and in August and September 1968 bed occupancy fell to 59.7% and 54.9%. Another crisis occurred in August when the Matron and the Committee Chairman interviewed the Night Sister about complaints they had received from patients. She left immediately, breaching her contract and leaving the Matron and other senior staff to cover for her. There were also several long-term absences among domestic and ancillary staff, and it was necessary to borrow a theatre porter from St. Richards.

A further source of frustration concerned a new sunroom built onto the women's ward. The workmanship was very poor, the roof leaked, there were draughts from ill-fitting doors and windows, several of which could not be closed and one pane of glass had been cracked during fitting and not replaced. The builder was severely censured.

Summary of work in the first six months of 1967 and 1968

	1968	1967
Discharges/deaths	91	74
Amenity (convalescent) patients	5	4
Operations in the main theatre	14	14
Other operations	2	20
Waiting list	2	4
Beds available	22	21.2
Occupancy	64.1%	80.6%
Average number of Patient/ bed	4.1	3.5
Turnover interval (days)	15.6	10
Average stay (days)	28.6	41.6
Outpatients	568	713
Outpatient attendances	1382	1406
Bacteriology	32	6
Chemical pathology	12	30
Haematology	31	23
Examination of surgical tissue	1	3
Exfoliate cytology (smear test)	7	0
Total pathology	83	62

The Community Hospital

In 1972 the operating theatre was closed and converted into a five-bed ward. Then in February 1988, a Rehabilitation Unit was opened, named after Dorothy Mitchell who had left a legacy covering a substantial portion of the £63,000 cost, with the League of Friends providing deep heat and traction equipment. The Physiotherapy Unit was now able to move to the Hospital from St. Ann's Hall.

But the largest change began on 4th November 1999 when an extensive upgrade of the Hospital, costing £1.9 million commenced. The patients were sent to the King Edward VII Hospital, while the physiotherapy department moved to Budgenor Lodge, courtesy of the Christ for the Nations Bible College.

The opening of the New Community Hospital was marked by an open day on 8th December 2000, which attracted several hundred visitors. It now had four multi-bedded wards, two single rooms, a day room and a purpose built treatment room, outpatient facilities, two consulting rooms, a physiotherapy department and a centre for meetings. People over 65 with mental health problems were accommodated in the new Pearson Unit.

Sadly, due to spending constraints, the Pearson Unit closed in 2006 in a year that also saw the loss of the King Edward VII Hospital. Despite fears for its future, it is to be hoped that the Community Hospital will continue to serve the area for many years to come.

Sources

The Community Hospital, Mrs Loo Rosser, and the Cowdray Estate for access to documents.

13.1   Rotherfield House stood in spacious grounds with a level terrace (left) and a lawn sloping down (foreground) to provide a splendid vista of the River Rother. The boat house was to the left.

13.2   Like many homes in 1939, the windows were sandbagged as a precaution against bomb blast. Being so high, the measure was of limited value and was never put to the test. Unlike Midhurst, there was no record of enemy action in the parish.

13.3   Rotherfield House could once be seen from the bridge at North Mill, but this is one of many village vistas lost by uncontrolled tree growth. The Rother Angling Club's ponds are in the middle area.

13.4   Rotherfield House is seen in November 2006, much extended as Midhurst Community Hospital. It is facing the Riverbank Medical Centre, which opened on 12th April 2000.

13.5   Behind Rotherfield House and thus seen by few is the Pearson Unit. Although the sign was still standing in November 2006, these assets were unused.

✎ 14. Conifers School ✑

Origins

Conifers School was founded in 1934 by Miss Barbara Gayford, with her sister Joyce, in premises in Egmont Road previously occupied by the Cottage Hospital. As a private school few records were kept and little information survives from the early days. School photographs taken in 1953 and 1955 and posted on the Internet, show there were about 44 pupils and six staff. In 2006, there were 80 pupils and 14 staff.

Miss Gayford was headmistress for 26 years and her successor, Mrs Helen Sproule, served a similar period. Mrs Jenny Peel followed in 1986 and Mrs Louise Fox in 2004. The school is now administered by a charitable trust with a board of governors.

Activities

The school is co-educational, catering for girls between two and a half and 11, and boys up to the age of eight. The youngest children are "Fir Cones" progressing to juniors and finally seniors.

There has always been an emphasis on music, drama and sport; the parish mgazine in the 1970s recorded annual carol services in the church and joint sport and entertainment days in summer. The original sports field was opposite the school, but when this became a car park, a new facility was opened on the other side of Easebourne Lane. Fencing and judo are taught as well as the usual sports.

A wide range of music is enjoyed including an orchestra, a swing and marching band and a drum clinic. There are clubs for art and computers, and even a breakfast club for the early birds.

14.1   This post card was sent in 1926 and thus shows the building when still in use as a hospital, also the conifers which gave the school its name. The neat hedge has spread considerably in recent years.

14.2   Class rooms were added at intervals, the nearest being the gymnasium in the 1950s. The latest is far right. Far left is the car park, which had been the school playing field until about 1995. This facility is now east of the main road (right) on the site of an infilled fish pond, the slight hollow of which often made an unofficial skating rink for villagers.

14.3   A prefabricated class room arrived on 3rd June 2006 and road closure was arranged for it to be craned into position on a Sunday morning. It was for use as a 6th form classroom, common room and changing facility.

15. A Tour of the Parish

15.1 Only pedestrians using North Mill bridge will see the clasped hands of the parish boundary stone. The most northerly of Midhurst's first street gas lamps was nearby, but the glass facing Easebourne was blackened so that it did not receive the benefit of any light. Hidden by the boards of the footpath (added in about 1950) is a stone marked 1776.

15.2 We start our tour at North Mill on 26th December 1992, when work had started on junction alterations that would allow provision of a mini-roundabout. Vanzell Cottage contains a stone dated 1666 and was the only habitation hereabouts for centuries.

15.3 Few bridges are regularly closed by floods when the river flows freely a great distance below. This is the scene on 11th October 2006 as contractors attempt to find the gratings, each of which was blocked by a few leaves. The main channels were occluded by other debris. Paving slabs on blocks are used throughout the world to solve such problems, but not here.

IX. The 1938 map shows the relationship of the southern part of the parish to Midhurst (lower left). The dots of the boundary are mostly in the centre of the River Rother, which is bridged by a path between the town and The Ruins. This historic approach is known as The Causeway, as it crosses marshy ground prone to flooding. An early abattoir was situated near the double bend south of North Mill on Hogs Blood field.

15.4 The ruins of Cowdray were crumbling towards total collapse by the end of the 19th century. This photograph was taken shortly before the first major restoration began in the Edwardian era.

155. The stables are dated as 1726; they were built southwest of The Ruins, close to the river for easy cleaning. They were photographed in about 1910 and were used for a dairy herd in the 1950s.

156. The conversion of the stables involved extensive alterations for the sale of anything other than horses. Two of the shops are seen in November 2006.

157. The granary stands between the stables and The Ruins, which were under renovation when photographed in 2006. The grain was protected from vermin by steddle or staddle stones, of mushroom-shaped configuration. The granary probably came from another Cowdray estate in the early 20th century.

15.8 A glider made a forced landing in Cowdray Park on 14th May 1995 without damage or injury. Rescue by road trailer was expected, but No! Within an hour, a small but powerful aircraft landed and towed it away, as light was fading.

15.9   Few know of Cowdray Heliport. It was busy on 20th July 2006 with polo visitors. Inset is the sock and H landing sign. The flight path is over the residential area, although open country surrounds it.

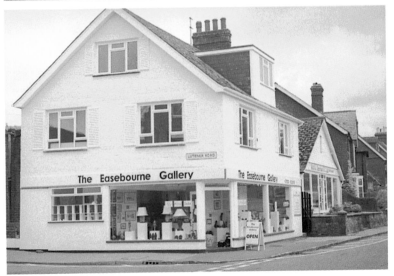

15.10   Gillhams shop and car showroom in Easebourne Lane subsequently served a variety of commercial purposes, notably as the Tile House for many years. The shop is seen subsequently, in July 2003, offering objets d'art from the Far East. RAK Ceramics was the next occupier of the buildings behind the shop, the firm specialising in bathroom furnishings from the Middle East.

15.11 Three cottages faced the west end of the church graveyard, after it was extended in 1915. The area later accommodated the war memorial. The building was converted into a single dwelling in 1933-34 and still belongs to the Cowdray Estate.

15.12 Difficult to identify now, this is the view east towards the gates of Cowdray Park from the north end of Easebourne Lane. The main road is obstructed by earth from the trench which is about to receive the pipes on the right. On the left is Snow Hill, then the residence of the Cowdray estate agent.

15.13 Every seat was occupied in St. Mary's for the Remembrance Day service in November 2006 and the subsequent ceremony at the War Memorial involved the traditional dipping of the flags of village uniformed organisations. A total of 60 from the village died in the wars.

15.14　　An account of a dispute in 1428 states that Midhurst church had to maintain parts of Easebourne church if it was to retain the right to bury its dead there. This included 72ft of the graveyard wall. Other churches without consecrated burial grounds were Lodsworth and Fernhurst. This is the boundary stone in the north wall between Easebourne and Lodsworth's responsibility.

15.15　　The boundary of Fernhurst's section of wall is to be found near the bus shelter. Demands are no longer made on neighbouring churches; a devoted group of local parishioners spent much of the Summer of 2005 repairing it themselves, mixing over two tons of mortar.

15.16　　This 2006 panorama is from the culvert of the Es Bourne and the low camera position shows how successive road makers have raised the A272 surface to the window cills of the Manor House. This dam impedes storm water flow to its natural course down Easebourne Lane and necessitates sand bags at the Post Office doorway. The stone facade on the timber-framed Manor House bears the date 1778.

15.17 The "White Horse" retains much of historic charm, both inside and out. Since the advent of repeated flooding, the main entrance has been closed and the gateway boarded up. Maybe a temporary renaming would bring some action: "The Suffer in Silence". The shrub on the right is on the site of the shop seen in picture 9.3 on page 100.

15.18 Glaziers Lane has few dwellings and thus little claim to fame, but this cottage is where a secret hide near the chimnney contained the 1603 Catholic service manual mentioned in the text.

15.19   Moving up Easebourne Street, we can enjoy the first of several well balanced Georgian dwellings. This is now the Old Vicarage reflecting its use until about 1910. It is listed Grade II*, the only building so treated in the parish.

15.20   Three cottages on the east side of Easebourne Street lost their thatch in 1921 and were subsequently known as Burnt Cottages. They are now simply C17, C18 and C19, a geographically random estate system of no value to the emergency services. They were reroofed with tiles and later listed Grade II. There is not a fireman in sight!

15.21 Recorded in the 1960s, The "Holly Tree" was a one-bar beerhouse, devoid of a car park. The road over Bexley Hill remained unsurfaced until the 1950s.

15.22 The most northern shop in the parish was Pearce & Son, just below the turning to Loves Farm. Beyond the lorry is the paraffin store, supplying customers without mains electricity. Pearce's homemade cider was kept in a store in the orchard behind the house and they supplied "The Duke of Cumberland", "The Rother Inn" and "The Plough Inn" at Redford.

15.23 Challens Yarde is on the east side of The Street and this is its west elevation when in use as a wheelwright's shop and three cottages. The timber is thought to be for wheel repairs. The timber framed structure is considered to be 17th century or earlier. Listed Grade II, the building's first floor at the rear "oversails on oak bressummer and brackets". Apparently this facilitated the lifting of waggons.

15.24   The National Grid does not supply the village directly, but its pylons stride across the parish from Dungeness Nuclear Power Stations to the West. Their construction was managed from a depot in the former goods yard at Rogate station in 1968. More recently, some power has come directly from a small plant using otherwise unusable gas from the oil wells at Singleton.

15.25   The seldom seen engineering marvels of the TV mast on Bexley Hill would appeal to many with artistic appreciation. The buildings have high security and are even devoid of door knobs. Having taken a south-north trip through the parish, we return to Cowdray Park. The final views are to the west and the northernmost part of the parish, Henley.

15.26   A view in the opposite direction from the "Byepass Bridge" has the lost cattle grid in the foreground, Cowdray Estate offices on the right, the lych gate of the churchyard on the left and the ancient Manor House centre. The vertical bars on its east elevation are of the type used at apertures to allow smoke to escape, before chimneys were invented. The road sign was provided by the RAC.

15.27   We have returned south to visit Cowdray Park and have our backs to the Priory. Thought to be the route taken by huntsmen to North Park, the location was ideal for concealing part of the military transport fleet used during the Dunkirk evacuation in 1940. Canadian troops from Aldershot later used the area for training for D-Day.

15.28   Moving east along the A272 to Benbow Pond, we see some of the square-styled saloon cars of the 1930s. The background is the location of the famous ancient oak tree, seen in the picture after next.

15.29 At a tranquil location on the east bank of Benbow Pond is the memorial erected after the death of Viscount Cowdray in 1995. The Autumn colours of 2006 added to the joys of the varied birdsong.

15.30 Known as the Queen Elizabeth Oak, this tree is reputed to have provided a shooting shelter for the monarch in 1591 and to be over 1000 years old. It has a girth of 41 feet and is close to the footpath which traverses the golf course. The shape is explained by pollarding, the removal of branches periodically.

15.31 Silt traps were built at the east end of Wick Lane; their width allows flood water speed to be reduced and this gives time for the suspended silt particles to drop. It reduces the mud on the roads, if the traps are emptied regularly.

15.32 Wick Lane sees very little traffic, as modern farm equipment is mostly too big for it. The tractor, pictured in November 2006 was towing a party on a partridge shoot, while another group further north in James's Quarry were after the pigeons. The sandstone and iron layers are evident.

15.33   The redevelopment of Budgenor Lodge was recorded on 6th April 2006; the main building would be clad with scaffold for over six months. The old highway enters the dark hole on the right, another water-cut route.

15.34   Also close to the crossroads is Dawsley Farm, or Dodsley Farm, one of the oldest buildings in the parish but, like many others, no longer part of a farm. The chimneys were probably retro-fitted to the timber-framed structure.

15.35 The cottage for the toll collector was on the south side of the crossroads. On the left was the pound for stray animals and also Wheelbarrow Castle, signposted as the road to Petworth.

XI.   The 1912 map of Easebourne Lane reveals the remains of the original course of the Es Bourne. Bridges are shown over it to every dwelling north of Lutener Road, where it was piped diagonally to the other side of the road. It is shown in the open a little further on where there was a grating, similar to the one to be seen near the post office. Most of the water had been diverted along the leat shown on the east side of the field adjacent to the main road since the 16th century. A glimpse of our early history can be had down a grating at the east end of Egmont Road - pure flowing water.

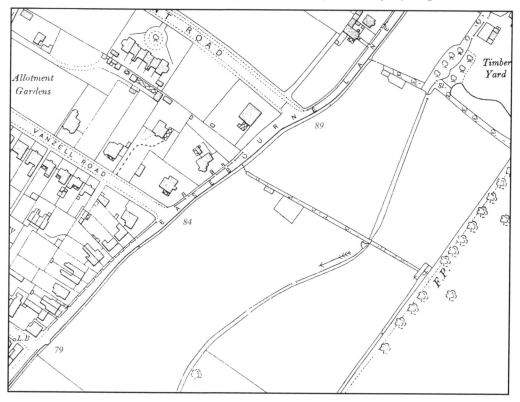

16. Henley

16.1   The "Duke of Cumberland Arms" is thought to be of 15th century origin and was recorded as a dwelling in 1726. It was used by a "beer retailer" in the 1860s. The name was that of the victor at the Battle of Culloden in 1746; this may be the origin of the name of the inn.

16.2   The 1885 Mission Chapel in Henley was the highest building in the village in terms of altitude. It is marked on map II on page 8. It had an association with a chapel at Bexley Hill until about 1913. St. Mary's Church still benefits from an endowment from the sale of Henley Chapel in March 1966. Ecclesiastical boundary changes meant that it had been in Fernhurst since April 1959.

16.3   *Ths shop at Henley was near the brickworks on Henley Common and thus just outside Easebourne parish. John Thayer was in business in 1886 and Thayer & Son trading in 1914 as baker and grocer and also running a sub-post office. The cottages still stand, but the postbox is on the roadside.*

16.4   *The Cowdray Estate owned most of the dwellings and land in Henley. It undertook the local water supply and erected this pump house in the early 20th century. There were (and are) numerous springs in the upper part of the village, where the water was filtered before being pumped to a reservoir on the ridge of the hill. The tower housed the steam engine and the pump was in the nearest part of the building, seen as a dwelling in 2006.*

❧ Postscript ❧

To many of the thousands of motorists who approach the village from the London direction on the A286 on their way to the coast, or to those who drive west along the beautiful but dangerous A272, Easebourne may well seem just a few scattered houses on the way into the traffic bottleneck of Midhurst. Even if they notice the name Easebourne they will almost certainly pronounce it wrongly! Or some child in the back of the car will say, "Dad, you've gone wrong again! We shouldn't be anywhere near Eastbourne." But to the discerning traveller whether from the north or the east, there are two major buildings which proclaim that there is more to the village than at first meets the eye.

High above the A286 is the stern profile of Budgenor Lodge, once a workhouse and now a prestigious housing complex with some 'affordable housing'. On the A272 as speed is suddenly reduced on a winding country road, a glance to the left reveals a picture postcard scene of Church and Priory behind a rolling lawn, with the edge of Cowdray Park stretching away into the distance. Each in its own way enshrines an aspect of this little Sussex Community whose story is told in these pages.

Of Budgenor Lodge, the very word 'workhouse', with its harsh Victorian ring, and the phrase 'affordable housing' with its overtones of a modern approach to the alleviation of poverty show how the outworkings of the social conscience have changed in the two centuries since it was built. Even as one reads through its history in these pages, words such as 'pauper' and the account of unbelievably difficult conditions jar one into the reality of how far we have moved. How totally different the Victorian aura of the workhouse seems to the 'caring' ambience of the present bustling Health Centre down by the River Rother which was opened in the year 2000.

But it is the Priory/Church complex that gives a much longer and deeper insight into the history of this parish. Inside the Church building itself, the remains, buried in the walls of one time arched doorways and windows, and the many memorials of those long departed, speak in a way which transcends mere words, of beginnings lost in the mists of time and of tortured change through the centuries.

The recently erected board giving the names of vicars stretching back to the Middle Ages poses almost as many questions as it answers. Was the Incumbent at the time of the Civil War evicted by the Puritans and later restored, as happened to so many? The name of the first recorded vicar dated 1276 is Norman French, one Peter de Wynton. What about the unnamed men who succeeded him before the first English name appears 125 years later? What would they make of us and of all that has grown up over the years from the humble foundations they laid?

The living community they founded still touches every level of village life. Its members meet in strength in the Church Sunday by Sunday and every day of the week in smaller numbers as their forefathers did, to worship God and to pray for the whole community which they serve in many ways. This extends from providing for all the treasured 'rites of passage' of christenings, marriages and funerals, to the managing and editing of the much valued village magazine 'United'. There are many other societies in this village, but by far the oldest, and even in this secular age, the greatest in numerical strength is the Church Community which uses these beautiful buildings.

All things alter of course, and the challenge for Easebourne in this new century is to bind up the wounds caused by the demise of the King Edward VII Hospital which after all only lasted for one century of the Parish's long history and to face the future. Many things change and will continue to do so. It was ever thus. If the story written in stone in the Priory Church of St. Mary's is anything to go by Easebourne will rise to the challenge.

Revd Norman Wyatt

Middleton Press books on northwest Sussex include

Betwixt Petersfield & Midhurst   Changing Midhurst
Branch Lines around Midhurst   Batttle over Sussex 1940
Blitz over Sussex 1941-42   Bombers over Sussex 1943-45
Secret Sussex Resistance   Sussex Home Guard

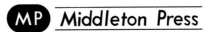

MP Middleton Press

Easebourne Lane, Midhurst, West Sussex. GU29 9AZ
Tel: 01730 813169   Fax: 01730 812601   Email: info@middletonpress.co.uk   www.middletonpress.co.uk